S0-BSM-683

HUMBLE YET FIERCE

HUMBLE
YET FIERCE

MY LIFE BEHIND
THE CURTAIN OF THE CIA

KATY MCQUAID

NEW DEGREE PRESS
COPYRIGHT © 2023 KATY MCQUAID
All rights reserved.

HUMBLE YET FIERCE
My Life Behind the Curtain of the CIA

ISBN   979-8-88926-941-0 *Paperback*
          979-8-88926-986-1 *Ebook*

Humble Yet Fierce is a work of nonfiction. The events are from the author's memory. Some names and identifying details have been changed.

The opinions expressed in this book are solely those of the author, and not of the CIA.

To Grace for helping me find my voice

Contents

———

Author's Note

—

When I was in middle school in the early 1970s, the only swim team was a boys team. Some of my girlfriends and I, with the support of our parents, lobbied to join it and compete in their meets. All I wanted to do was be on a team and race. I didn't care if I was competing against boys, including my older brothers. Surprisingly, the school agreed to let us join, and we got some life lessons to boot. Despite being a team and having the same objective—namely, to beat other teams—our contributions did not seem to be appreciated, particularly if they involved over-shadowing our male counterparts by beating them.

Boys who lost to a girl were teased: "You've been BBB'd," i.e., Beaten by a Broad. It made me extremely uncomfortable, particularly if it was me they had lost to, and especially if it was one of my brothers. However, I didn't have the courage to speak up and stop it. Instead, I internalized my feelings; they became a pit in my stomach.

I applied to the Central Intelligence Agency (CIA) in 1983, right out of college. The labor market was tight, and receiving no better offers, I accepted theirs. Working at the CIA proved to be like being a member of the boys swim team, right down to the pit in my stomach during the early years of my career there. Reflecting on it now, my experience in middle school was the beginning of my ability to successfully work in a man's world.

As was typical at the time in the CIA, men had most of the power and influence. This meant I had to put in longer hours, work harder, and handle more responsibilities. There wasn't much tolerance for failure from women, meaning it took longer for me to recover from a mistake than for my male colleagues. A male manager who interviewed me during the hiring process said, "Logistics is hiring more women than men" because "you women will get pregnant and leave."

A 2013 report, "CIA Women in Leadership," headed by former secretary of state Madeleine Albright called for "significant reforms." It found the CIA culture failed to sponsor and promote female officers, which "directly and negatively impacts the mission" of the CIA. The report indicated women made up 46 percent of the CIA's workforce, up from 38 percent in 1980. Female representation at the general service (GS)-13 to GS-15 levels had increased from 9 percent to 44 percent over the same period. The CIA compares well against our Intelligence Community (IC) counterparts and private industry. As of October 2012, females constituted 31 percent of the Agency's Senior Intelligence Service (SIS) officers (CIA 2013).

While these overall statistics show real progress, the leadership pipeline for women at the CIA narrows above the GS-13 level for most directorates. Agency-wide, female officers account for 43 percent of GS-14s and 37 percent of GS-15s. The 2012 SIS promotion process resulted in 19 percent female promotions to the SIS—a concerning difference from the 30 percent-or-higher average of female promotions since 2007. If the 2012 outcome were to be repeated in the coming years, such a trend would lead to diminishing representation of women at the senior ranks.

When I started at the Agency, I may have believed, like many women still believe, that I was limited by my gender. Living and working in a male-dominated organization wasn't always easy, but I learned **the only one who limits you is you.** Yes, career growth as a female can be slower, and it may take more effort to break those gender barriers, but it can be done.

I started out as an entry level GS-7 logistics officer. Like a 2nd lieutenant in the Air Force or Army, an "officer" in just about name only. Accepting demanding overseas assignments and managing increasingly large supply chains and the workforces necessary to accomplish the missions they supported, I progressed into senior executive (SIS) positions—the equivalent of a general in the Air Force or Army—leading large global support operations. I was the CIA's first female logistics supply officer promoted to SIS. I was the first female and the first SIS chief of support in Afghanistan. By being good at what I did, not only did I break self-imposed barriers I held about myself due to my gender, but I also shattered the glass ceiling put in place by a male-dominated culture.

I've been an avid student of leadership, behavioral science, and psychology my entire life. I started by emulating my parents, teachers, and coaches and going to the library to read any book I could get my hands on about the topic. I was a natural leader from a young age. People gravitated to me for advice, counsel, and leadership even in my early teens. I'm not exactly sure why this happened, but people sense I truly want to see them succeed. I want to know what motivates people so I can help them flourish.

I carried this desire to serve the greater good when I worked at the CIA. The CIA is like any other organization: there are some good bosses, some great bosses, and some not-so-good bosses. I watched not-so-good leaders and knew I didn't want to lead the way they did. They taught me what *not* to do. These leaders typically used their position to command followers. I took every opportunity to learn from the good and great bosses with whom I worked. I could see their positive impact on missions and on the individuals who worked for them, myself included. I took notes because I wanted to have the same influence as a leader.

I learned effective leaders don't have to be loud to be strong. In fact, people who are humble yet strong and courageous are often the most effective leaders. Indeed, recent studies have shown these attributes make the difference between a good and a great leader. A humble leader stays true to their purpose and leads from their heart.

A study by Catalyst (Prime and Salib 2014) states humble leadership has the same positive influence regardless of gender or nationality. "Humility was one of the most significant indicators, after empowerment, of altruistic leadership" in this study. The study also found that, regardless of business or country, humble leaders make their employees feel included, making them more comfortable in proposing innovations and helping others.

Many of my former colleagues are some of the most intelligent, caring, and selfless people I know. They make personal sacrifices in service to each other and the country, repeatedly. The CIA isn't a place for loners. Relationships, trust, and teamwork are essential for success. An important aspect of working there, for me, was the relationships and lifelong friends I made.

This book captures a look at life in the CIA from someone who worked behind the scenes in logistics and global support operations, from driving on dangerous roads in remote villages to closing a CIA covert facility to my experiences in war zones. The stories will engage you and anxiously have you turning the pages, wanting to see what comes next. I also share personal stories highlighting 1979, the year that defined me professionally and set the foundation for my life.

An important part of my story includes the journey to find my voice. I showed courage in many ways, but speaking out wasn't one of them. It took me over fifty years to find the courage and comfort to speak up and be seen, which brought me to write this book.

Humble Yet Fierce is for you if you're at a point where you want to try something new, are at a crossroads, or need to make a decision you've been putting off. Perhaps you're entering the workforce for the first time, recently divorced, or in a mid-level position and need encouragement to take your next steps. Hopefully, this book will help you find your voice and the courage to move forward with grace.

We all have a story, and it is our story that defines our values and how we show up in life. I won't call my experiences good or bad, but I do believe they all happened *for* me—they didn't happen *to* me. The significant life experiences of my youth gave me the mental, physical, and emotional stamina to prepare me for the challenges I would face in the CIA and made me who I am today.

I hope my stories will inspire others to know they can be successful even when they don't fit the mold.

PART 1

HUMBLE LEADER FROM THE START

Early Influences: Competitive Swimming & Personal Loss

———

There's nothing like the feeling of achievement in a moment of adversity. I love it when I'm part of a team that wins. The pursuit of this feeling inspires me to persevere even when things get difficult.

I first learned that about myself through competitive swimming, which I began at the age of seven, almost by accident. It was 1968, and in response to the USS Pueblo being boarded by North Korean forces, my father's Air National Guard unit in Niagara Falls, NY, was activated, and he was sent to Lackland Air Force Base in San Antonio, TX, taking my family and me with him. Seeking to ease the pain of our temporary displacement from our longtime home and friends, he signed us up for the swim team on base.

I proved to be pretty good, and competitive swimming became a huge part of my life over the next fourteen years. Progressing from a community-based team in the Buffalo area to the nationally known Solotar Swim Team in Northern Virginia that had produced Olympians, and eventually Penn State, I experienced teammates who were goofy, mischievous, and smart, and who dared to be different and were very dedicated.

I remember having fun with my teammates in practice at local and regional meets and ultimately at the Amateur Athletic Union (AAU) Nationals. Yes, there was a lot of alone time spent looking at the black line at the bottom of the pool. Plenty of time was also spent in between sets when we caught our breath and analyzed how we were doing or how we motivated each other to get through a difficult set or practice. And let's face it, in a pool full of boys and girls, many of us had secret crushes on each other.

The most fun was when it was a team accomplishment and I played a part in it. That's where I thrived. I liked to help my team succeed and win. I enjoyed high-fiving my teammates and loved the feeling of joy when my relay won. I hopped out of the water and jumped up and down with my teammates, while my arms and legs tingled, and I cheered at the top of my lungs with a wahoo or a loud whistle perfected over the years.

As a kid, I was shy and inwardly confident, always having a drive to work hard and be good at whatever I did, but not outspoken, willing to let my actions speak for themselves. Moreover, I wanted others to succeed, and apparently, my shyness didn't prevent that from being perceived. A coach once told me that people sense my innate desire to help them, telling me, "Katy, you're just a natural leader. When you walk into a room; people can feel your presence, strength, and courage." Another mentor said, "There's something about you; people feel it, but they can't figure it out." That personality also led me to seek and be elected my high school class president my sophomore through senior years.

I learned while swimming for Penn State that I could lead the team in practices through my sheer grit and determination. I gave it my all in practices, and it contributed to the team, but I never achieved the level of success I hoped for as a Nittany Lion.

THE ROAD TO PENNSYLVANIA STATE UNIVERSITY (PENN STATE)

By my junior year in high school, I was a reasonably accomplished swimmer and believed I had the potential to be offered a scholarship, and began visiting several colleges with that in mind. I'll never forget one of my 5:00 a.m. practices when Coach Solotar asked me to get out of the water to talk with him. "Katy, have you considered looking at Penn State?" I told him, "No, it's not on my list." He said, "You might want to think about it." He explained that Penn State was building its women's swim program, the school was good academically, and it was only a three and a half-hour drive from my home in McLean, Virginia.

I had an outstanding year my senior year in high school. I qualified for Senior Nationals and the Olympic trials in the 200-yard breaststroke. That swim happened in a time trial at the US Naval Academy pool. It was my best time ever, and it launched interest in me from several Division 1 (D1) schools.

Penn State's coach, Ellen Perry (EP), invited me up for a campus visit, and my mom and I got to stay at the quaint Nittany Lion Inn on campus. It was wintertime with snow on the ground, and the swim team was in season. I got to meet prospective teammates and watch a meet.

As we drove back to Virginia, I said, "Mom, I really loved Penn State." The campus was beautiful, and I got along with the swimmers who showed me around campus. I also trusted Coach Solotar's opinion that it would be a good fit for me. Penn State quickly became my number one choice.

As much as I wanted to go to Penn State, it was going to be a financial challenge. I would be an out-of-state student and couldn't afford to go there unless I received a scholarship. I had offers from three other D1 colleges and couldn't justify going to Penn State without one from them. When a white envelope with the Penn State seal eventually arrived in the mail, it was thick, which I took as a good sign. I called my dad at work and said, "Dad, there's a letter from Penn State in the mailbox."

He said, "Well, what does it say?"

"I don't know. I'm shaking too much; I can't open the letter," I said, and we both laughed as I opened it. There it was: a full scholarship, including tuition, room, and board. Penn State, here I come!

I could barely wait for summer to finish so I could move to Penn State and start swimming for the Lady Lions. As I packed, I envisioned many things, but none of them prepared me for what would come next.

PERSONAL LOSSES

As I was getting ready to leave for college, Jean Rachner—one of my coaches at Solotar Swim Team, to whom I was very close—suffered an aneurysm when driving home from practice one day and collapsed in her driveway. In a coma and on life support, it was a miracle she survived.

Making my final preparations to leave for Penn State, I visited her in the hospital. She had withered down to sixty pounds; it was hard to see her in this condition. It broke my heart. I cried as I held her hand and thanked her for all she had done for me. I believed she could hear me. Before I left her room, I kissed her on her forehead and said goodbye, realizing it was probably the last time I would see her.

I completed all the shopping a new freshman does before leaving for college, getting new sheets, a comforter, and a plastic bin to carry my shower supplies to and from the bathroom. My dad teased me before he drove me to PSU, saying he was going to open the car door and "leave me on the curb." Teasing me was his way of covering up how difficult it was seeing me go off to college. Of course, that didn't happen. When I got to Penn State, we unloaded the car, and he and my younger brother went with me into my dorm room. My dad had tears in his eyes, and he got choked up as we said goodbye.

I was sad the first few nights I spent in my new dorm room. I laid in bed at night, looking at the springs on the bunk bed above me, and wondered how long it would take to make new friends. It was a big change for me—new routines, new teammates, new coaches, and new experiences. It didn't take long, and I started to adapt.

I called home one night after returning to Penn State after a short Thanksgiving break, and my dad answered the phone. As we were talking, I said, "Dad, I'm really happy. I love it here."

He said, "You know, Katy, I always knew you would make the right decision where to go to college."

My euphoria wasn't to last. One week before Christmas, I came back to my dorm from swim practice, looked up at my dorm room window as I approached the building, and saw my roommate looking out. She quickly stepped away from the window when she saw me. As soon as I walked into our second-floor dorm room, she handed me the old black rotary phone with a cord plugged into the wall. As I put the receiver to my ear, an old family friend was on the other end, and he told me my father had died of cardiac arrest. He was forty-eight years old.

Within minutes, Coach EP arrived at my dorm room with Sam, one of my high school teammates. EP said the roads were too dangerous to leave right away, and she would drive me home first thing in the morning.

I was in shock. I remember lying in bed that night, and my body was shaking; it felt like I'd placed my fingers in a light socket. The next morning, when I put on my normally tight-fitting Calvin Klein jeans, they were so loose they fell off my hips. I shivered so much overnight I must have lost ten pounds. As EP drove me home, I sat in her car's front seat, hugging a pillow, helplessly trying to fight back the tears that wouldn't stop. I wasn't prepared for this.

We had my dad's funeral a few days before Christmas. Family and friends came from all over the country. Because my dad was in the Air National Guard, an honor guard played Taps, complete with a 21-gun salute. The day was gray and overcast, with a cold that chilled me to the bone.

I went back to Penn State after Christmas break, but I really didn't want to be there. I wanted to stay home and help my mom and my younger brother, who was still in high school. When I told my mom I wasn't going back to school, she insisted I had to because that's what my dad would want. It took a lot of courage for me to go back to school. While I loved being at Penn State, it wasn't yet home, and it certainly wasn't conducive to dealing with grief and loss.

Within weeks of my return, President Carter announced the US was boycotting the 1980 Olympics. It was hard to imagine being any more deflated than I was; my dream of going to Olympic trials and competing for the US team had vanished overnight. Moreover, the pain was compounded because I felt so alone and did not feel I had anyone who could truly empathize. My mom was dealing with having just lost her husband, and Coach Rachner, who had always been there for me in the past, was on life support. Therefore, I was left to internalize the deep pain of an unfulfillable lifelong dream.

I don't think my coaches at Penn State knew how difficult it was for me. Within months of turning eighteen and going off to college, I lost all my points of reference. A mentor on life support, adjusting to Penn State, my dad dead, and an opportunity to compete for the Olympics gone. A friend of mine used to say, "What doesn't kill you only makes you stronger."

I could only hope that was true.

Not surprisingly, I didn't swim well that first year. I was extremely dedicated in practice and worked hard. But when it came to meets, I choked. As hard as it is to believe, my practice times were often better than they were in meets. I put a lot of pressure on myself, but nothing I did changed the results. As a full-scholarship athlete, the standards were high, and I couldn't meet them.

Returning home after my freshman year, I wasn't motivated to work out. I went to practice, but things were very different. Jean wasn't coaching, and I would visit her at her home, but I couldn't spend much time with her because she was in physical therapy and focused on her recovery. Besides, what was there to train for without the Olympics?

I returned to Penn State in the fall of my sophomore year at least twenty pounds overweight and not in great shape. But who cared; there were no Olympics. There was pressure from my coach to get the weight off. In fact, my teammates and I were required to weigh in every day, and our weight was recorded on a large printout by the scales in the natatorium. I was defiant at first, but eventually, the public humiliation motivated me to get back into shape. We also had a change of coaches. EP stepped down as the head coach, and her assistant, Coach Robert Krimmel (Krim), replaced her.

This change was significant because there are high expectations when a D1 school hires a new coach. Coach Krim needed his team to win, *and now*. The limited number of scholarships he had to offer was his primary means for achieving that end. Desperate to keep my scholarship, this put intense pressure on me. But I still couldn't meet expectations when it came to meets. I would break school records in practice and choke when it really counted. I went to the NCAA swimming championships a couple of times during my four years at Penn State but never stood on a podium. Nonetheless, I retained my scholarship. It wasn't until the awards banquet of my senior year that I knew why.

There, Coach Krim noted my role as a leader in practice and how I pushed my teammates to new levels. No one ever doubted that I was dedicated. I worked my ass off. But there was something psychological blocking me from producing in meets. Looking back, I could have really benefited from counseling.

How different would my life have been had my dad had a more normal life span? I have no way of knowing. I do know his death changed the course of my life.

PERSEVERANCE & COURAGE

I really wanted to give up at the end of my freshman year, but the courageous part of me wouldn't let that happen. Many times during those four years of swimming, I was embarrassed and ashamed that I couldn't produce at the level I thought possible.

Looking back now, I realize those challenges set the foundation for my life and the ability to work through tough times. I had to trust myself and persevere; it took a lot of courage for me to keep showing up, and I did. I never wanted to let my teammates and coaches down.

It took me about three years to overcome the grief of losing my dad. I walked around campus with a heavy heart. I didn't know how to process the sadness until, one day, I was standing by the checkout counter in the bookstore at the HUB (Student Union Building), and there was a "Best of" *Dear Abby* book.

In my mind's eye, I can still see it clear as day, sitting in the rack near the checkout line, a narrow, red-covered hardback. To this day, I am convinced it was no accident I was in that line. Randomly opening the book, I landed on a page where the question was about grieving. "What is the appropriate amount of time to grieve?" the person asked. Abby's answer was to grieve if you want to, but it's a choice when you decide you're going to let go of it. At that moment, I said to myself, "You've grieved long enough. It's time to get on with your life." Simple as that. I had to pivot. Forget swimming greatness and the Olympics. Accept that Dad was gone. It was time to move on.

As my graduation approached in the spring of 1983, the US had still not recovered from a deep economic recession that had begun in 1980. The job market for graduates like me with newly minted BS degrees in finance was very tight. Of the few opportunities that presented themselves, the one I thought would be a dream job was director of planning for special sporting events at Penn State. Logistics, event planning, and large sporting events (think NCAA championships) were all things I enjoyed. I cobbled together a résumé and applied because, if successful, I wouldn't have to leave State College, Pennsylvania. I didn't get the position.

Interested in seeing me move on, my mom kept bugging me to get my résumé so she could give it to a family friend who was the CIA's deputy director of logistics. The friend told her they were on a hiring blitz for logistics officers and specifically looking to increase the number of women employees. I didn't want to go work for the CIA at the time. It was hard to imagine it would be interesting and fulfilling. But it is hard to tell my mom no. Thank God for persistent mothers.

Now, it's hard for me to imagine working for any other organization could have been as interesting and fulfilling.

CHAPTER 1

My First Tour (Southeast Asia: 1985)

Six months after graduating from Penn State, my security clearance came through, and in December 1983, I began working at the CIA. It was no secret I was going to be stationed overseas. The question was, where was I going?

Junior logistics officers typically spent twelve months in a structured training program learning the basics of Agency logistics. With the yearlong training under our belts, my colleagues and I were ready to receive our first overseas assignments.

Seeking some advance notice of where we might be headed, some fellow junior officers and I went to the Vienna Inn on a Friday night in December of 1984. We knew some of our bosses would be there, and we hoped to gather some intelligence. Despite its name, the Vienna Inn is a local dive several miles down the road from the CIA headquarters at Langley.

It's a local hangout where customers enjoy the loud clanking of dishes, talking over the jukebox, the smell of chili dogs, and feet sticking to the beer-stained floors. Sure enough, Tim, one of the logistics division's senior managers on the assignments panel, was there. He was so excited about my first posting that he shared the good news with me before my official meeting with the director of logistics, scheduled for the following Tuesday.

He said, "Katy, Southeast Asia, you're going to love it! The weather is warm year-round, and there will be lots of men because there is a Naval Base and Airbase nearby."

That's how employee development worked in the old days and how the CIA works in general. Relationships, trust, and a beer are usually involved.

Despite Tim's enthusiasm, all I wanted was an assignment in Europe. I was quite stunned by the news but tried not to let it show on my face. I thought, *I applied to seven positions in Europe. Surely I'm not going to Asia!*

The CIA operated a logistics hub in Europe with a large team of logistics officers stationed there. Every logistics officer wanted to be stationed at that post. There were plenty of reasons for that: teammates, military mail service, good food, Christmas Markets, shopping, and it was easy to travel throughout Europe.

And truth be told, when I got home that evening, I had to pull a map off my bookshelf to ensure I knew where I was going. At the time, there was some upheaval in the region related to countries transitioning to representative governments. Wanting to ensure elections were peaceful, free, and fair, the US, along with Asian Pacific partners, established sites that would enable them to respond quickly to any tumult. Thankfully, I learned about my new assignment on a Friday night. I had three and a half days to think about it before my official meeting. And think about it I did.

I was being assigned to an unstable area halfway around the world from my friends, family, and everything I knew to a place with hot weather year-round. I thought, *What am I going to do without four seasons and my beloved Fair Isle sweaters?* Not to mention, the flight was twenty-four hours one way, there was no internet at the time, and it cost ten dollars a minute to call home. That was expensive, especially as a GS-7 officer. It would not be easy to stay in touch with my friends and family, and I didn't know a soul there.

In the three and a half days of thinking, I came to my conclusion. I was going to simply tell the director of logistics, "I'm not going." But something happened. As I drove to work that Tuesday, there was a voice in my head that said, "GO. This is what you are supposed to do."

And somewhere between my car and the director's office, I decided to **step out in faith** and accept my first overseas assignment to Asia.

Of course, there was plenty of opportunity to second-guess my decision as I went through the permanent change of station (PCS) process. It took eight months to complete the training I needed and get my household effects and car shipped.

The PCS process entails taking courses to prepare one for their overseas assignment. I was required to take the CIA's weapons training, cultural awareness, additional logistics training, and the "crash and bang" driving course, where I learned defensive driving techniques.

I didn't grow up with weapons in the home; this was all as new to me as learning to drive a car in a hostile environment. I was interested in learning something new, but it also reinforced the seriousness of the situation where I was going to live.

During my processing, I thought, *What am I doing?* A tug-of-war went on in my head: "You can still back out, Katy! No, you can't. Yes, you can!"

Then a crystal-clear voice came into my head and said, *Have faith, Katy, just have faith.*

On the day I shipped out, I arrived at Washington National Airport in my Penn State preppy best, a bright pink Land's End cotton blouse with navy-blue chinos. I wanted to look professional but also wear comfortable clothes for the twenty-four-hour flight, and appropriate for the hot and humid weather I would encounter upon arrival. It was time to say goodbye to my mother, brothers, and some friends who came to see me off. I was very nervous, and as I tried desperately to hold back the tears, I hugged everyone and said my goodbyes.

After twenty-four hours of being crammed into a tiny airline seat, I finally landed in Asia. My stomach twisted into knots, and my mind in a fog, having nothing to do with an after-midnight landing, I navigated the hustle and bustle of the airport. My sponsor and her husband met me there and drove me to my hotel. The unfamiliar smells and loud noises of the city overwhelmed me, and the air was thick with humidity.

I checked into my hotel, and my sponsor planned to pick me up for brunch the next day. I'd never met Mickey before, but she was one of those people I connected with immediately. She gave me the lay of the land and helped me get settled into my living quarters, I am grateful to her to this day. And it seemed like heaven.

I was assigned to a two-bedroom apartment for my tour. I was excited to have a place of my own for the first time. My veteran colleagues thought the apartments were dumps. But as a newbie to this life, I disagreed and enjoyed my cozy apartment on the second floor of a three-floor white brick building. As I walked to my place, I passed a pool and a lovely courtyard with green palm trees that swayed in the breeze.

My apartment and office were on a compound across the street from a large bay. It was a convenient way to live, with a short walk to work and lunchtime workouts in the pool.

Six weeks after I arrived, a record-breaking typhoon came through our location. I had never experienced such heavy rain and wind in my life. It was a Category 5 typhoon with 140–175 mph winds. The sound of torrential rain beating down on the windows, pavement, and cars parked outside my window kept me awake all night.

My car was in transit on a ship somewhere out in the South China Sea, which meant I had no choice but to walk to work. I was such a rookie I didn't think to call the office and ask for a ride, so I decided to walk to work that morning. I thought, *I must get into work.*

Donning khakis, a green cotton shirt, and white leather slip-on shoes, I made my way across the compound, trying to get to the warehouse where I worked. The rain was so fierce that when I stepped out my front door, the umbrella I was carrying immediately turned inside out, making it completely useless. I continued down the stairs to the ground floor and stepped into water so high it was above my hips. I couldn't see my feet through the water, and the rain was coming down so hard it was painful to keep my eyes open. I slowly put one foot in front of the other, feeling the ground beneath me so I wouldn't slip and fall.

As I walked across the compound, chairs, tables, debris, and palm fronds swept past me. The water was moving swiftly as it got deeper and deeper. It took all my strength to move forward and not get swept away.

I made it into the office, soaked to the bone. I wasn't good at asking for help in those days, so I improvised. I went into my office, closed the door, stripped off all my clothes, and placed them in front of the standing floor fan that was there to cool my usually stuffy office.

When my clothes were somewhat dry, I put them back on and went out to the warehouse. The warehouse crew was busy sewing sandbags by hand to place by all the doors and windows. They were doing all they could to save our critical inventory from being ruined. I'd never experienced anything like it in my life, and I realized it was the beginning of learning to do things a new way.

A few weeks later, as my officemates and I were recounting the typhoon experience, one of the admin assistants said, "Katy, I thought you were alone in your office because you were homesick and crying. I didn't realize you were butt naked, trying to dry your clothes!" I had to laugh. This was the start of a new adventure where I learned to adapt, accept, and admire my new surroundings. My life was filled with new sights, smells, traffic, and poverty like I'd never seen before. It was eye-opening and fascinating.

That being said, I couldn't wait for the mail to be delivered each day, because I wanted to hear from people at home. A special package arrived shortly after my arrival.

A group of my sorority sisters sent me a "birthday in a box." They held a party in Virginia to celebrate my twenty-fourth birthday and packaged it up and sent it to me. The package included photos from the party, a piece of chocolate cake with chocolate frosting, a previously lit blue and white candle, and an assortment of gifts. The impact of their thoughtfulness was profound.

I realized I could be halfway around the world and my friends were still with me.

It took me about six months, and suddenly, it felt like Asia was home. I figured out how to drive my car in the notorious Asian traffic. Motorcycles weaved in and out with horns honking as pedestrians randomly crossed the road, and men offered to clean my windshield with rags as I sat at a red light. Driving in Asia is an art form. I also adapted to the relentless heat and humidity, which included taking two showers a day. It really felt like home because I had begun to build a routine that included eating ramen noodles and getting my nails polished on Saturday afternoons. I've since coined the phrase "Home is where my pillow is."

I'd read a Navy study about culture shock and the process one goes through when they move to a new country. The study outlined the significant events and physical, behavioral, and emotional responses one could expect. The study concluded that it takes six months to feel settled after a move. And sure enough, it was like magic.

I lived and worked in Southeast Asia for nearly four years. During my stint, a revolution occurred, which was a series of popular demonstrations in 1986. Nearly two million people took to the streets, ending a twenty-year dictatorship and restoring democracy.

One night, I worked my way through the crowd of over two million protesters to get to work at the control center. I was filled with a sense of awe as I walked through the crowd, realizing these people were standing up for what they believed in and making their voices heard.

When I arrived for my shift, Senator John Kerry—decorated Vietnam War veteran and future Democratic candidate for president—was standing in the control room. He was one of several US politicians and senior government officials who traveled to the country to monitor activities and facilitate the transition. He grabbed my arm and said, "Come with me. I need someone who knows this city to accompany me to a church where the poll workers refuse to continue to work because they witnessed voter fraud and anomalies."

Accompanying Senator Kerry gave me a firsthand look at a senior government official reacting under pressure to uncertain circumstances. He was confident and graceful in his handling of the situation. I watched Senator Kerry adroitly handle the press as he met with the poll workers to address their concerns. On our drive back to the control center, he shared his thoughts on the electoral fraud and how he was going to report it back to Washington.

What I remember most from this experience is the women who were working the presidential elections polls. They witnessed voting irregularities and had the strength and courage to stop counting until their concerns were addressed.

This was an incredible learning experience, and it was an opportunity for me to **step out in faith**. The situation went on for three days, coming to an end when the deposed president agreed to exile. Hunkered down in my apartment at night on the phone with a friend who was responsible for loading families and their belongings onto a US military aircraft, I said, "Tom, tanks are rolling down the street next to my apartment, and it sounds like the helicopters flying overhead are going to land on my roof."

He replied, "I just helped load those helicopters."

I learned about faith when I was twenty-three years old. That first step onto the airplane to Southeast Asia in 1985 shaped my future. It took a lot of faith and courage, but it led to thirty-two incredible years with the CIA, living and working around the world. Faith is an integral part of who I am and how I operate. Faith is what guided my career decisions and allowed me to stay true to myself and my values.

CHAPTER 2

Individuality
(Southeast Asia: 1986)

—

My first overseas assignment was also my first experience managing a group of adults. It was also my first true immersion in a male-dominated work environment.

As in the military, CIA personnel have a "rank." I was the only female "officer" at the station and a junior one at that. I was responsible for activities related to stocking and distributing warehouse goods. That included managing a workforce comprised of (non-US) locals. Despite my official rank and the latitude to get the job done, efforts required teamwork, and many employees had worked in the warehouse for years. Being humble was in order, and humble I was. Indeed, being open to them in this manner was highly beneficial to me, affording me the opportunity to learn about their culture and what was important to them.

That being said, the job was challenging. Things didn't always go as planned, and for mission-critical activities, problems had to be resolved quickly. In such circumstances, I had to walk fine lines, deferring to those with more experience yet speaking up and taking action when I thought they were wrong, or I had a better idea. I tried to be "one of the guys" while maintaining my femininity.

To put some distance between me and my job, I sought relationships and activities with people outside of the CIA. Because of the overlap between their missions and logistics considerations, some overseas CIA offices are proximate to other US government agencies and non-government organizations (NGOs) such as the Peace Corps and groups attending to refugees. This made it easy to get involved with activities outside of the office. I made friends in embassies, US Navy Jag Corps, and several NGOs, and slowly developed my own routine. I went to Jazzercise classes and taught water aerobics in the community.

My fondest memory is scuba diving, which I managed to do with an amazing group of smart, dedicated, and fun colleagues three out of every four weekends the last two years of my tour. We loaded our scuba gear in our cars on Saturday mornings and headed to a small fishing village a few hours away.

There, we hired local fishermen to take us out on their boats and typically made three dives per day. The village staff prepared delicious meals of fresh fish and vegetables before we sat by the fire and shared stories for the evening. Nighttime meant sleeping under mosquito nets in thatched roof huts and waking up to roosters crowing at the crack of dawn. Many of us have remained lifelong friends.

Early on, this didn't go over particularly well with the men in my office. One colleague started giving me the cold shoulder, so I asked him, "What's up?" He said, "You never join us in the pub for beer after work anymore."

Another time, I was in the office on a Saturday morning with the other managers. We were attending to a crisis in one of the countries we supported. The boss called me into his office and said, "Why aren't you in here *every* Saturday like the rest of us?" I responded, "I'm here if there's a need, just like today. Have I ever not been here if there's something going on? I won't be here just to be here."

They didn't know that was who I was—and am. In college, I was the first Penn State Lady Lion Swimmer to join a sorority, Kappa Kappa Gamma (KKG). The women's swim team was very close-knit, and no one had ever joined a sorority before. That knowledge made me reluctant to wear my KKG letters at first. But I slowly got comfortable wearing my sweatshirt around the swim team and talking about my activities in the sorority.

"I wish you could have joined me for the KKG Balloon Derby Fundraiser," I told some teammates. I grinned as I described the rush of excitement walking on the perfectly manicured field during halftime at a Nittany Lion football game.

Being in a sorority expanded my circle of friends, social opportunities, and put some distance between me and the "job" of swimming. It proved to be contagious. The next year, three more women swimmers joined a sorority.

My first overseas assignment reinforced the importance of maintaining my individuality and a reasonable work-life balance. It can be difficult. Superiors may have unrealistic and even counterproductive expectations, and trying to meet them has the potential to lead to group-think and/or burnout, not to mention denying oneself the great joy of true friendship and new experiences.

CHAPTER 3

Learning on the Fly (Southeast Asia: 1987)

———

The vibrant colors of red, green, orange, and blue were everywhere as I kicked gently with my flippers and listened to the hum of air coming through my regulator. Scuba diving in the South China Sea was spectacular. There was nothing as peaceful as swimming around coral reefs, clown fish, octopuses, moray eels, shipwrecks, and even sharks. It was serene and beautiful, until it wasn't.

Our group had some diving experience under our belts and decided to charter a dive boat to go on a special diving excursion over President's Day weekend. It was a large houseboat with a suffocating smell of exhaust fumes. Dive tanks and our gear were stored in the back of the boat.

The first day of diving was beautiful, with calm waters and plenty of sunshine. We were out in the water, about a mile from the shore. Our dives included some of the most colorful reefs and fish I'd ever seen.

On the second day of our trip, I volunteered to go ashore to help one of the divemasters get provisions for the day, including food and ice. While we were on shore, the rest of our group went on their first dive of the day. When I got back to the boat, I noticed my friends weren't on the boat and asked, "Where are they? How come my friends aren't back from their dive?"

The captain said the divers were planning a shallow dive, and so there was no need for concern because they could be underwater for a long time. I knew something was off. Even if they were going on a shallow dive—which means their air tanks lasted longer—they'd been gone far too long. I knew my friends well, and their tanks would be out of air by now.

I demanded we begin a search for my fellow divers. This wasn't as easy as it sounds. The captain thought it was unnecessary, and he also knew that if something went wrong, he would have to answer for it.

I continued to insist we begin a search. I looked the captain straight in the eyes and, with all my resolve, told him, "We must begin to look for my friends. I know their air consumption rates, and there is a problem."

A divemaster got into a dinghy with one of the boat hands, and they began to search for the group of divers. They came across two divers, Jonathan and Lee, who were trying to swim to shore to get help. When they returned to the dive boat, they described to me what had happened.

The group went down for the dive, and the currents were extremely strong, and the divers got swept away from their starting point. As hard as they tried to stay stationary, the current moved them swiftly away. The boats that were supposed to pick them up weren't in the right spot, so when the group came to the surface, they drifted out to sea. Jonathan and Lee were okay, but the rest of the group was still somewhere out at sea in shark-infested waters.

Jonathan and Lee took a dinghy onto the shore and asked the local fishermen to begin searching for our colleagues. Fisherman after fisherman replied, "Sorry, sir, we don't have any gas." The guys ended up bribing the fishermen with $100 to search for our friends. Suddenly, the fishermen got in their boats and started their search on the choppy waters.

Jonathan also found a local businessman who knew the area well and understood the tides. He said, "Your group went into the water at the wrong time. They should not be diving at 9:00 a.m. because that's when the current shifts, and it is very dangerous because the currents are at their strongest." My friends were adrift at sea because the boat crew led them into the water at the wrong time.

We called the US Embassy via the boat's radio. The embassy alerted the US Navy, which began an official search and rescue operation. The waters kept getting choppier, and there was no sight of our friends. The sun started to set as the Navy's helicopters flew overhead.

The vessel was completely silent except for the static coming from the onboard radio. I felt helpless as I stood on the side of the boat, looking over the choppy water at the horizon, with the hope of spotting the others. I prayed, "Please, God, just show me a pop of color from their dive gear. Please help us find them and keep them safe."

Jonathan and Lee were so angry they stood in front of the rack with air tanks and started to throw them over the side of the boat. I heard *kerplunk* as Jonathan muttered, "This isn't fair. How can the rest of the group still be adrift at sea?"

Just as the sun was going down over the horizon, two small fishing boats approached our boat. My prayers were answered; some of our friends were on board. Seven people found, two more to go.

As we lifted our weary colleagues onto the boat, there was a bustle of activity. They were cold and shivering, and most were crying. They needed to talk and tell us what happened. We wrapped them in blankets and towels and hugged them as tight as we could. They were safe, but we had two more people out there. The tension grew as the sun dropped below the horizon.

Thirty more minutes went by before a fishing boat pulled up to our boat carrying the last two divers—Preston was on the fishing boat with his teenage daughter.

None of us slept that night as we recounted the events of the day. While everyone was safe, we were extremely lucky. The group drifted ten miles in shark-infested waters that were ten thousand feet deep. I learned the importance of knowing the capabilities of my teammates. Had I not been aware of their skill level and realized something was wrong, the search would have been delayed and the results could have been very different. We also learned the importance of bringing in an expert for the area. If not for the local shop owner who knew the tide table and predicted where the tide carried the divers, it could have meant the loss of life. Thankfully, his knowledge of the sea brought us the safe return of the group.

I also learned how important it is to bring in professional help in the case of an emergency. The arrival of the Navy and embassy resources to help with the search and rescue was critical, as were the mental health experts who came to assist with individuals who experienced trauma. The outcome was successful because of their support.

Throughout my time in Asia, I valued the interactions I had with the locals, whether that was telling me about warehouse operations or protecting the warehouse during a major typhoon, or by giving me the information that saved my diving friends. If I hadn't learned to listen and communicate in a way they could hear, my friends would have died. If I hadn't stood my ground to be the voice for others, my friends may have died. Looking back, one thing I've noticed was that it was easy to find my voice for others, and even easier in extreme situations. I only wish it was that easy when I needed to do so for me.

PART 2

JUST SAY YES

CHAPTER 4

Just Say Yes
(Southeast Asia: 1993)

——

"Just say yes" is a motto I've lived by, and it's served me well.

In 1994, I was the CIA's logistics (logs) officer in another Asian capital city, working from the station. The station had several bases, one located near the border. My boss came into my office one morning and said, "Katy, I need you to close out a base on the border." I didn't have to think about it, and I just said, "Yes." It was a base filled with rich history—one chronicled in movies and books. I was excited I had the opportunity to go there.

The base was a beehive of activity back in the day, supporting special operations, and it included multiple warehouses, office space, group living quarters, and special facilities for operations gear. It was important the US turn over the buildings to the host country in clean and operating condition. All the equipment needed to be dismantled and properly disposed of. Was this a glamorous and sexy operation like you'd see in a movie? No. But it was essential and had to be done.

I was lead for the effort, and I was the only American on a small team of foreign nationals—or locals—tasked with closing the base. I was grateful for my team of locals. They were vetted and had a long history of working to support our operations. Ms. Sang was our head local employee, and she had run the warehouse for decades. Ms. Sang knew how to get anything done. She could have easily stayed back in the office and not gone on the trip. Instead, she advised, "Ms. Katy, I plan to go on the trip with you. It's a big job and I want to help."

I knew enough about where we were going to know the most dangerous part of the assignment was going to be driving over narrow, treacherous, and winding roads to get to the base. The long drive—which took all day—was on two-lane roads where small cars, such as Toyota Corollas, played cat and mouse and zoomed to get around trucks on the road, only to do it again when the next truck was in front of us. I saw my life flash before my eyes at least ten times on the way there, and we witnessed numerous serious accidents along the way. Unfortunately, driving was the only option for getting to the remote village.

I think the drive there took ten years off my life. Thankfully, and with a lot of prayer, we made it safely.

The special program we were shutting down had been gradually slowing down for years, and by the time our team arrived, it was like a ghost town, with doors creaking and empty water containers scattered about. I was struck by a hollow feeling as I looked at the empty and desolate spaces. It certainly wasn't what I'd seen in the movies, and I could only imagine what it was like during the height of its operations.

We got right to work when we arrived. Everyone instinctively knew what to do as they had worked together as a team before. I was technically "the boss," but that was a misnomer. It was the team of locals who were really in charge. They knew what they were doing. There were four warehousemen who started packing the heavy machinery and equipment. Ms. Sang surveyed the living quarters and commented, "There are many things to take care of here." We rolled up our sleeves and started by clearing the kitchen.

I winced as I looked at the dust and mice poop everywhere. The closeout involved packing up everything from antennas, typewriters, automobiles, machinery, and radio gear to kitchen appliances and dishes. It was a dirty job, and someone had to do it. I felt bad that Ms. Sang and the team of locals had to endure the dirt.

I got to know the local staff well because we lived and worked together on this project for a couple of weeks. It strengthened my bond with Ms. Sang. We set up cots with light sheets to sleep on in one of the old buildings that had running water, and we bought most of our food on the streets. Truly, this was an incredible way to learn about the culture. In addition to getting to know the locals well—and them me—my language capability improved, and they made sure I ate well.

I'm all about the food, and the locals recommended dishes and often did all the ordering when we ate from local food stalls, noodle carts, and restaurants. I am an adventurous eater on my own, but the team knew the best spots, and they made sure I didn't miss any delicacies. As we shared meals together, they often commented, "Ms. Katy, you are a good eater; we like it because you eat spicy food." I experienced some of the best food that was unique to this part of the world.

I was always with the team during this project. We worked together, stayed in the same house, and ate meals together. There wasn't time for me to be alone. I had to adjust to this because I'm someone who likes my alone time.

As much as I wanted to complete the job, I was *not* looking forward to the drive back to the city. But it turned out to be okay. Again, I just said, "Yes."

Shortly after the base closeout, I returned to the station, and one of the locals who was on the trip invited me to an Asian pop concert. There was a popular female singer who was at the top of the Billboard charts in Asia. Her songs blared from every radio station in every shop and restaurant in the city, and she was a pop icon who couldn't walk down the street without the paparazzi following her.

I didn't have to say "yes" to the concert, but, of course, I did. I was excited to experience a concert with their beloved star.

What I didn't realize until shortly before the concert was I was going to be seated at a table that included members of the

Royal family. It was a *big deal* to be sitting with members of the Royal family because there is so much protocol involved. The princess was highly respected and well known for her work with disadvantaged youth. She also had a reputation for being more reserved, less splashy than her siblings, and she traveled with a small entourage.

I was nervous, so I began finding the right clothes to wear. It was essential to find the right outfit and jewelry. I trusted Ms. Sang, who suggested I "wear a silk skirt and top with special jewelry." Ms. Sang approved my outfit made of shiny teal and gold silk with 24 carat intricate gold earrings, a necklace, and a four seasons bracelet.

Next, I started asking questions about protocol and what I could and couldn't do. There was a lot to learn about royal protocol and a few adjustments needed to be made quickly. I took deep breaths to calm my nerves as the Royal family approached the table. Once I calmed myself down, the rest of the evening went smoothly. I remained seated when the princess came to the table. The conversation was light, with the princess mostly interested in my family. "You grew up with four brothers? What was that like?" And I was allowed to look at her when talking because I was a westerner, but locals were not.

The concert was held in the grand ballroom of an elegant hotel. The large room sparkled, and it was filled with a hum of excitement throughout the night. The food was wonderful, and the audience waited with anticipation for each song. It was a very special evening and one I will never forget.

I enjoyed the music, the food, and the company. It was a once-in-a-lifetime opportunity to sit with members of a royal family and listen to the concert. Her version of Bette Midler's "Wind Beneath My Wings" was dedicated to her father, who was sitting at my table. There wasn't a dry eye in the house.

Just saying yes to that invitation created a fantastic memory and a moment of culture I wouldn't have experienced had I said no. That moment and many others like it happened because my motto while working at the CIA was "Just say yes." I learned early on that no two days were alike, and I also knew that "saying yes" would lead to new opportunities. One day I could be holding on for dear life driving on dangerous roads, cleaning up mouse poop, and the next I could be attending a concert with a Royal family. One thing is for sure, saying yes kept opening doors.

Shonda Rhimes talks about the power of *one* word, "yes," in her book "Year of Yes." Shonda Rhimes is an American television award-winning creator, producer, and writer of *Grey's Anatomy* and *Scandal*. She committed to saying yes to all things that scared her, and she said it changed her life. In her words, "Saying yes undid the fear and made it not scary." She also talks about how saying yes opened her up to new challenges, invited collaboration, empowered others, and made life more fun!" (Rhimes 2015).

Shonda Rhimes wrote her book the year I retired from the CIA, and she wasn't wrong. I just said yes because I knew it would lead to possibilities I couldn't imagine.

Every story was the result of just saying yes. Every yes brought in new people, new places, new cultures, and unique experiences, which is exactly what happened when I became the first female deputy director of logistics.

CHAPTER 5

Opportunities and Risks (Langley to Afghanistan: 2003-2006)

———

I became the deputy director of logistics (logs) in 2003. It was an assignment in which I was asked to take the position because "logs is broken." The director of logistics asked me to apply because he said, "I need someone with your strong leadership and organizational abilities to help clean up the mess."

At the CIA, I had a reputation as a fixer, someone who could turn around a troubled organization, start a new capability, or manage a large global organization on a moment's notice, often in a foreign field. I didn't think of myself this way until I realized being a fixer was required in many of the positions I held as a senior officer. I enjoyed the challenge, and it turns out, I was good at it. One of the reasons I'm good at it is I can see the big picture and see the steps it takes to get things done. I am strategic and tactical at the same time.

I moved into the deputy logistics position at a hectic time in the Agency. In 2003, logistics support was struggling to meet increasing demands for logistics officers in conflict zones. In addition, we had to keep the normal worldwide logistics operations running smoothly.

The director of logistics and I were sending large numbers of logs officers into the conflict zones. Many of them were young officers with young families. I was in the deputy director of logistics position for about two years when the CIA's directorate of support was having difficulty filling the senior support position in Iraq; no one volunteered to go. Other senior officers declined the position due to personal reasons, such as kids in high school, the demands of the job, or simply the desire to stay in their existing headquarters (HQS)-based positions. The likely candidates to fill the position said no. When I heard this, I said to my boss, "Bill, I think I should volunteer to take the senior support position in Iraq that no one is applying for."

He said, "What, are you crazy?"

I told him, "We are sending so many junior officers to the conflict zone, one of us in a senior position needs to step up and lead by example." I think my exact words were "We can't sit here fat, dumb and happy" and ask the others to make a sacrifice we aren't willing to make. I thought it was a perfect opportunity to show the logistics workforce that their leadership was willing to do what we'd been asking of them.

It turned out the executive director of the Agency (EXDIR) got involved in the decision of filling the position. It was unusual for him to be involved at this level, but he was a field guy. He liked to keep his finger on the pulse of support positions in conflict zones. I don't know all the details from the EXDIR's conversations with the director of support (DS), but the DS said she fought hard to make the Iraq assignment happen for me. Ultimately, the EXDIR recruited one of his guys to fill the position.

While disappointed I wasn't selected to go, I leaned on my faith and said, "This is happening for a reason."

Shortly after the Iraq chief of support position was filled, the DS called me and asked if I'd be willing to go to a different conflict zone. She planned to upgrade the Afghanistan chief of support, a mid-level manager position, to a senior executive position. "It's time," she said. The Agency needed to start building infrastructure for the long haul in Afghanistan. It was a big deal because there were very few senior executive support positions in the field, and the Agency was serious about upgrading its infrastructure in Afghanistan.

"Katy, you were willing to go to Iraq. Are you willing to go to Afghanistan?" the DS asked.

"Of course," I said.

During the initial phase of the conflict, the Agency's setup was expeditionary in nature. Officers lived in sea—aka shipping—containers and huts made from human feces. When it rained, the smell was so pungent, it was overwhelming and made me queasy. Officers slept on cots in the motor pool. Communication packages used to send information securely were tactical. Generators were undersized and unable to keep pace with the growth of the mission. The list went on.

Because of this, the DS decided to put a senior executive in position to manage and right size the support operations and infrastructure across the country. She wanted someone she could count on to deliver.

Truth be told, I was so happy I ended up where I did. I'd been to both war zones for short visits, and I preferred the atmosphere in Afghanistan. It was gritty, fast paced, and most importantly, it was new. The systems, infrastructure, and processes in place were already set up in Iraq. I was going to have the opportunity to create and build from the ground up with the support team in Afghanistan.

It's part of my faith; I believe not going to Iraq was divinely orchestrated so I could go to Afghanistan.

I remember talking to the Agency's deputy director of security shortly after my assignment. I said, "Hey, Pat, I need to get into the crash and bang course soon so I can be prepared to drive when I'm in the conflict zone. It's been a long time since I went through the Agency's hazardous driving course."

Pat looked at me with this funny look and said, "Katy, when you go to Afghanistan, you won't be driving... you will have a security detail with you at all times when you are moving off of the compound."

I can be very independent and afraid to ask for or accept help when it comes to me. I intended to drive myself during my new assignment. I thought I would challenge him on this point and then I reconsidered, thinking, *Maybe I will keep quiet.* I realized he was the security professional, and I would take his advice.

This was another fast turnaround assignment, and I quickly got organized. Every permanently stationed officer was required to carry a weapon, which meant I had to go to an intense training course. It had been many years since I was certified to carry a weapon.

I came back home from my week-long weapons training and packed up my things. I was on a plane within a month. When I arrived, I made it my number one priority to visit all the forward operating bases (FOBs). The FOBs were an important part of the station's operational activities located outside of Kabul. I wanted to see firsthand the living and working conditions and figure out how best to support the people working there. This was a time of transition.

Travel to the outlying bases involved flying in a helicopter under the cover of darkness. My favorite part of these flights was catching up on sleep. I'm good at sleeping on any kind of aircraft, and a helicopter is no exception. I would sleep on the helicopter even with door gunners, night vision goggles, and the cold thin air at fourteen thousand feet. When we arrived, the base personnel waited on the tarmac to meet the flight, which delivered cargo and people.

On one of my first base visits, the helicopter arrived at a remote one, and the chief did a double take as I got off the helicopter. The base personnel were shocked. I remember him saying, "We've never had a chief of support visit us, let alone a female chief of support."

I experienced another base with austere conditions. The toilets the guys were using were built out of plywood and kitty litter. The stall door was supposed to lock with a hook latched through a ring... but it didn't. The base was all men, so they didn't think anything of it. There was *no way* I was going to leave the door open to go to the bathroom. I wasn't going to have them walk by while I hovered over the makeshift toilet. I giggled and shook my head as I placed one hand on the door, trying to keep it closed, and the other trying to keep my weapon from slipping off my belt and into the hole with the kitty litter.

This situation reinforced why I visited the bases. I wanted to see firsthand the living and working conditions so we could create a thorough facilities infrastructure program. It was desperately needed.

One night, I was getting off the helicopter, and dust was flying everywhere. I traveled with a group, and there was a guy there to install new communications gear. As he stepped off the helicopter, he shook his arms in the air and yelled, "I can't believe I get paid to do this."

I smiled and thought, *I feel the same way.* I was honored to be doing interesting work and serving my country on such an important mission. I enjoyed the fast pace and the opportunity to stretch outside my comfort zone and learn new things. Most importantly, I was part of an amazing team doing meaningful work that was aligned with my purpose of serving the greater good.

When I accepted the position as deputy director of logistics, it came with opportunities, and it came with risks. By just saying yes, I was propelled into a position with increased visibility and exposure at the senior levels of the Agency. It was a double-edged sword, but I was glad I didn't back down from the challenge. Working in Afghanistan provided me the opportunity to work in a complex environment where it takes a team to successfully complete the mission. It further reinforced for me that trust is a must-have for a team to work well together.

CHAPTER 6

Traditions Not My Own (Southeast Asia and USA: 1995, 2008)

———

It was a very hot day with a warm breeze, and I was in the middle of a field in a remote part of Asia. I was there with our foreign counterparts to discuss possible locations for a new antenna to help with the transmission of radio signals. Our counterparts were so surprised this "white woman" made the trip out to the far reaches they rolled out the red carpet for my visit. They were very generous people, and they made sure to treat me like royalty. I appreciated their attention to protocol, and it was something I never took for granted.

The temperature was at least 95 degrees with 90 percent humidity as we got ready for lunch. Out in the middle of nowhere, we sat at a table set with a blue linen tablecloth, nice dishes, and cloth napkins. "Miss Katy, we made our very special soup for you." They were so proud of the meal they were about to serve me. I was honored to partake in it. The soup they were serving was considered a delicacy. It looked like chicken broth with pieces of skin floating in it with blanched almonds on top.

Experience had taught me it was better to eat without asking, but I had to know. So, I asked the commander, "Sir, what is in our very special soup?"

He replied with a grin, "Shark gut soup."

That was worse than I was expecting, and with a slight hesitation replied, "Oh, sir, I am so honored that you are sharing this delicacy with me." I continued to eat the soup one spoonful at a time.

My instincts had been correct: Sometimes it was best not to ask.

There were other times in my career when I had to adapt to the local customs. It's important not to offend the people you're working with in intelligence. While these instances happened regularly overseas, it also happened in the United States.

I was traveling in the Southern United States when I had to adjust to the culture in a situation where I wasn't particularly comfortable. This time also involved eating a meal, but it wasn't about the food.

Personal security training over the years taught me to never sit with my back to the door. Not only was I trained to think that way, but years of working with special ops types reinforced that behavior.

"Katy, face the door. That way you'll see what's happening and who is coming in a room."

I try to adhere to it even today. I like to face the door when I'm sitting in a restaurant; that way, I can see what or who is coming my way.

I was responsible for arranging a visit of the Agency's new EXDIR to meet with local law enforcement. He was an intelligent guy, down to earth, and low-key in terms of pomp and circumstance while traveling. He asked to have lunch with the state rangers because he wanted to learn about their operations and capabilities. "Katy, just find us a place to meet that's simple and where we can have a private conversation."

State rangers are law enforcement agencies responsible for investigating serious crimes ranging from murder to political corruption. They are also involved in specialized programs. While I'd never met them before, I'd seen enough about them in movies to know they are the tough guys and top tier law enforcement.

I scoped out several restaurants and found one in a small town with a private room for the EXDIR's lunch. I was concerned about finding an appropriate venue for the lunch. It needed to be discrete and secure. The security of the EXDIR was important, and I knew the state rangers would want to be careful too. I thought it would be a perfect place to meet because the restaurant was off the beaten path and the food was highly recommended.

We arrived in this little town via a gravel road, leaving a cloud of dirt in our wake, and parked our large vehicles. It was a hot day and there I was, walking down a dusty road with six strapping tall state rangers and the EXDIR. I don't know if it was the cowboy boots and ten-gallon hats they were wearing, but they seemed so tall. I'm just guessing, but they must have a height minimum to be a state ranger.

We arrived at the restaurant, and there were eight seats at the table for our group. I knew the rangers were *not* going to have their backs to the door, and I didn't want my back to the door either. One by one, the state rangers sat down after the EXDIR took his seat, and two chairs remained. I was still standing along with one lone ranger.

Everyone started to laugh, and not a word was spoken. They knew neither of us wanted to sit in the chair with its back to the door. I knew it was going to be me. You might say it was a dining room standoff. I thought, *Katy, there is no way the last state ranger will have his back to the door. Just relax. Who better to have eyes on the door than six rangers?*

That's why it is said eight law enforcement agents can never fit at a round table. Nevertheless, the barbeque was delicious and our meeting successful.

To this day, I will never forget the experience of being with some of our nation's most capable law enforcement, nor will I forget eating shark gut soup in the middle of nowhere. It was a matter of showing respect, and an opportunity to build the trust that was essential for building teams and strengthening relationships. When I said yes and accepted the cultures and traditions of others, it led to open communication, teamwork, and, ultimately, accomplishing the mission.

CHAPTER 7

Life Changes
in An Instant
(New York City: 1990)

———

A friend wanted to fix me up with one of her friends. We were having dinner after our scuba diving lesson, and she suggested I meet a colleague she knew through her position at the US Embassy.

"Katy, he's a great guy, lots of fun. I think you two should meet."

Sean Healy was a Navy lawyer in the admiral's office at the Naval Station in Asia, not far from where I was stationed.

Sean would occasionally come to the city for business, so I agreed to meet him. I am the naturally shy type, so I suggested we meet during a group get-together. The city had great live music, so we met at a club with a band. Six of us gathered outside the club, and as I approached the others, I knew right away who Sean was. He looked Irish, just like his name. He was tall and lean, dressed in a white-collared shirt and blue jeans. His hair was dark, and his eyes were blue. Actually, only one eye was blue; the other was brown.

The club was dark, with neon blue lighting, and it was so loud, I had to shout to be heard. It was hard to have a conversation. I had a great time listening to the music and dancing with the group. We became fast friends, and the next thing you know, we were walking out the door as the sun was coming up.

Our ears were ringing from the loud music as we stood by our cars discussing where to go for a late-night breakfast. Our eyes met while we were eating eggs with toast, and we shrugged our shoulders and said, "Let's just be friends."

We acknowledged the chemistry wasn't there, but we could have fun together.

Sean regularly came to the city with a couple of his friends for weekend getaways. They wanted a change of scenery, and I welcomed the laughs and time with friends. We would get together with other friends of mine for dinner, listening to music, and having great conversation. The guys slept wherever they could find a spot in my apartment. We usually finished the weekend eating burgers with chocolate shakes and hanging out by the pool. Sean and I developed a deep friendship during our time together. Those years I spent in Asia wouldn't have felt like home without him.

Sean had a *big* heart. He regularly volunteered at an orphanage for blind children, and he volunteered feeding the poor before traveling to Calcutta to work with Mother Teresa in her home for the gravely ill. He once pushed through a crowd outside a Yankees' game and administered mouth-to-mouth resuscitation to a homeless man suffering a heart attack.

This is how Sean lived every day. He was selfless and genuinely cared about others. I had a lot to learn from him.

ADJUSTING TO LIFE BACK IN THE STATES

We returned to the States within months of each other. I went to work in Langley, and Sean left the Navy and went to work in the Bronx as an assistant district attorney. We kept in touch and made occasional trips to visit each other.

One of those trips was in January 1990 when I was in New York City. It was a freezing cold night, and there was snow on the ground. After dinner, Sean and I went to see the newly opened Broadway play "A Few Good Men," a story of military lawyers at a court-martial. The lawyers uncover a high-level conspiracy while defending their clients, two United States Marines accused of murder. Sean had a few choice things to say about the accuracy of the military proceedings depicted in the play.

It was my first time seeing a Broadway show, and what better way than to see it with Sean and a story that was closely aligned with his work. It was a fun night, and before he took me back to my hotel, he insisted on showing me his new office at the Bronx District Attorney's Office on E. 161st St. He described how cars could only park on one side of the street for half the day, so someone in the office had to go out at lunchtime and move their cars to the other side of the street.

I could see my breath as we drove in his *new* car, filled with gas fumes and a defroster that made loud noises. As we got close to the building, my heart started racing and I felt queasy.

"Sean, I don't have a good feeling about where your office is. It doesn't feel safe to me."

He replied, "Katy, this is where I grew up. There's nothing to worry about. It's my home turf."

MAKING PLANS FOR LABOR DAY

We were finalizing plans for Sean to visit me in Virginia over Labor Day. I was looking forward to his visit because we hadn't seen each other in months. I needed some laughs and surely Sean would provide them.

Just days before his scheduled visit, my phone rang. As I picked up the receiver, I heard his brother Patrick's voice. "I don't know how to tell you this, but Sean died yesterday." I was in shock as my body started to tremble, and I shook my head in disbelief.

"This can't be."

"Katy, it's hard to imagine he's gone. Sean was killed by a stray bullet that hit him in the head as he bent over to buy a dozen donuts in the bodega across from his office."

Sean lost the coin toss that determined who would move the cars across the street at lunch that afternoon. On his way out the door, one of his colleagues suggested he pick up a dozen donuts.

My heart really hurt; it was broken into pieces. The grief and shock were like when I learned my dad had died. Only this time, it was my closest friend who was only thirty years old.

Sean's funeral was in a large church in the Bronx, and by the time I arrived, it was bursting at the seams with people waiting outside. It was a standing room only service with more than one thousand mourners attending his funeral.

A LIFE WELL LIVED

In a testament to the impact Sean's life had, one of his eulogists was New York City Mayor David Dinkins. In typical Irish tradition, the evening was spent in a local bar after the funeral. The place was something I'd seen in the movies—dark wood, low lighting, tough waitresses, and lots of history. Friends and family stayed in the bar until closing time, telling stories of who Sean was and how he made the world a better place.

I stayed in touch with Sean's family for many years. Keeping in touch helped me work through my grief and sadness. I felt called to visit his father, who lived alone at the time. It was a bit awkward at first because I didn't know the family well. I only met them at the funeral. That uncomfortable feeling didn't last long, and I visited Sean's father a few times.

One of those times was for the dedication of Healy Field. Sean was an avid baseball player in his youth. In honor of a life well lived, the city dedicated a ball field in his name in the Woodlawn neighborhood where he grew up.

This was the second time in my life I had lost someone close to me without warning. It shaped me. I realized every day is a gift, and I needed to live and not take life for granted. Life can change in an instant, and because of that, I just say yes. When opportunities come my way, I trust they are there for a reason. I say yes because I may never have that opportunity again, and who knows where it can lead.

I said yes, and it created opportunities to connect with people and create deep friendships with people who showed me how to be selfless. Saying yes taught me life can change in an instant and it's important to live each day to the fullest.

PART 3

TEAMWORK

CHAPTER 8

Teamwork Under Pressure (Persian Gulf: 1991)

Working and leading at the CIA meant coming up with answers to problems that couldn't be found on the internet or in textbooks. And finding those answers usually involved teamwork.

I've been on teams my whole life, and they have worked well for me. My teamwork approach to life started because I grew up with four brothers. We worked together to get things done as a family. I also participated in numerous team activities through high school from being a Keyette (service organization), a member of the Solotar Swim Team, and as a three-time class president. Teamwork continued to be an essential part of who I was as a Penn State swimmer and during my career in the CIA.

I was on assignment in the Persian Gulf shortly after the first Gulf War, and it was a typical hot, humid, and sandy day. My boss came into my office and said, "Katy, I need you to figure out how we can get some special gear to a team that is being held at gunpoint in a parking lot."

I was a junior officer at the time, and I had never encountered this situation before. How *was* I going to get communication gear to hostages who were being held at gunpoint? I knew the mission was important and lives were at risk. It was crucial to get the gear into the hands of the hostages so we could extract them safely. The boss was looking to me to come up with a solution, and it was all new to me. There was no instructional manual for this.

This is where my job as a CIA logistics officer came in.

I walked down the hallway of our makeshift office in an old dilapidated building, soliciting help from my colleagues. I needed their help to brainstorm ideas on how we could get the special gear into the hands of the hostages. The equipment needed to be disguised so it wouldn't be discovered by the militants holding them.

The team bounced ideas around, and we ultimately decided to disguise the gear to make it look like humanitarian supplies. We thought our plan was sound because it used international regulations to serve as the grounds to let the box in. They couldn't say no. The hostage takers were required to let the hostages have basic first aid equipment. We decided to give it a try.

My first step was to find the perfect sized box, one big enough to house the equipment. Finding a box was easy because there was lots of trash in the streets.

The next step was to find red and white paint and brushes to disguise the box as a first aid kit. This involved going to the local souk—or market. I ventured out to the market on my own, and the traffic was so congested it was difficult to cross the street after getting out of a taxi.

The souk was filled with stalls of vendors, along with loud sounds of motorcycles and people hawking their goods. The locals were selling everything from ornate rugs to head-scarves to bolts of fabric, jewelry, food, and over-the-counter medicine. It was like a flea market in the US, with a lot more noise, heat, unique smells, and crowds. As I searched from stall to stall for paint, I was invited in for hot tea with lots of sugar in it. There was so much sugar that it hurt my teeth. "Ma'am, please come in and look at my rugs," the men would say. Drinking tea is a custom in the Persian Gulf. I would look at rugs, drink some tea, chat a bit, and move on to find a stall that sold paint.

What would normally take me thirty minutes at Home Depot took me the better part of the afternoon, but I found the paint we needed.

I made a stencil to look like the red cross on a first aid kit and painted the heavy cardboard box. Once the red and white paint was dry, I loaded the equipment in the box, along with rolls of toilet paper, first aid kits, Band-Aids, gauze, and various toiletries to cover the urgently needed gear.

I painted arrows on the box that said "this way up" so if it was inspected, they would only find the supplies. Then I carefully closed the box and sealed it with heavy duty tape. It was a *beautifully* disguised box.

The operation took a great deal of coordination with the powers that be at CIA headquarters (HQS), which is also known as Langley. They asked, "Will the box pass inspection?" This and about fifty other questions had to be answered before we were given the operational go-ahead.

HQS approval came. Then the boss asked, "Who is willing to go on the helicopter to deliver the box?"

I raised my hand and said, "I am." I didn't hesitate to say yes because I trusted and had confidence in the helicopter crew and in my teammates who arranged every detail of the operation. I knew my teammates had my back, and I had theirs.

The stakes were high, and we got into sync quickly and moved with the quiet hum of a well-oiled machine. Every second mattered, and much like a race car pit crew, each person was focused on their part, and the handoffs were seamless. Lives were at risk, and we needed our special operation to succeed so the hostages could be brought out safely, and they were.

There is a strong bond and high level of trust that comes with this type of collaboration and brainstorming across teams. We thought through every detail and challenged each other with what-if scenarios.

Award-winning author and leadership teacher Simon Sinek says, "A team is not a group of people that work together. A team is a group of people that *trust* each other" (Sinek 2012).

My disguised first aid kit story is a perfect example of when I had to work out a problem with teammates and come up with a solution that couldn't be found in a textbook. I learned time and time again at the CIA that the best solutions came when teamwork was involved. Problem solving in the CIA was satisfying because I did it with others. I also learned trust was a critical element of any team I was on, never more so when the stakes were high and the pressure was on.

CHAPTER 9

Trust in Your Team (Afghanistan: 2005)

We often think about leadership as a title or about the people in our chain of command. But if there's one thing I learned as an Agency officer, it's that leadership isn't a title; it is a way of living.

A career as an Agency officer extended beyond the workplace. My colleagues and I lived and worked together, which meant I had little privacy. It was much like the C.S. Lewis saying, "Integrity is doing the right thing, even when no one is watching." In this case, though, it was also doing the right thing *because* people were watching. I learned early on that I was leading no matter where I was. Leadership was simply part of day-to-day life, and it went beyond what I was doing in the office.

I volunteered to go to Afghanistan as the senior executive responsible for support operations. The position held a "hefty title," but don't let that fool you; being the chief of support required humility and a willingness to roll up my sleeves. There was no corner office or plush living quarters that came with the position.

To give you a little background, the support chief's team is responsible for everything from security to logistics, armored vehicle maintenance, keeping the generators running, maintaining fuel supplies, medical care, and housing to meals, air operations, and secure communications. Basically, support is responsible for anything it takes to keep the station running safely and securely.

You may have gleaned that the CIA's main office in a country is called a station, and the smaller offices in the country are called bases.

When I arrived on site after an all-night flight on an Agency jet, I went straight from the airport to the station in an armored vehicle with my heavily equipped security detail. I walked into the new office, which was an old hotel bathroom with the original white tiling, floor drain, and that chilly feeling to it. I shared my new 10'x6' office with my deputy. My *plush* living quarters, which we affectionately called our hooch, was a twenty-foot sea container that I was fortunate to have solo, a perk that was provided to anyone on a one-year assignment.

As soon as I arrived, someone said, "Katy, the executive director (EXDIR) is on the secure phone, and he wants to talk to you." My first crisis and I hadn't even taken a shower. The EXDIR called me because the station was running short on critical supplies, and he wanted me to do something about it right away. I had a lot of experience and connections in this area, so I engaged former logistics teammates to get the ball rolling to resolve the issue as quickly as possible.

The problem was complex, and it required coordination between numerous Agency elements to solve it. I was overwhelmed by the severity of the situation and took a step back to catch my breath. At first, I wanted to hunker down and hope "this too shall pass." And then I reminded myself, I've done this before, and I can do it again.

That was life as a leader. No pointing fingers, saying, "How did this happen?" "How did our supplies get perilously low?" Nothing about "I need to sleep, I've been flying for a full day." Although I'm sure my officemates wished I'd taken a shower. I needed to figure out a solution, and I immediately engaged the support team to make it happen.

When I felt confident we had a good plan in place to get additional supplies to the station, I breathed a sigh of relief and went downstairs to the chow hall to grab some food and a cup of strong black coffee.

I wasn't back upstairs in my "office" more than five minutes when I was notified that one of the CIA's foreign service national—local—employees had died from a heart attack.

Local custom dictated that a senior official delivers an envelope with money to cover funeral expenses to his grieving widow—that someone was me.

This wasn't as easy as jumping in my car like I was in Northern Virginia. No, it meant getting back in the armored vehicle; this time, I had my weapon, body armor, and a different set of bodyguards to escort me to the deceased employee's home outside of the city. Our movement was considered a high threat situation because we were going outside "the wire" and into the outskirts of Kabul. We were driving into an unfamiliar area, and we didn't know who was friend and who was foe.

We arrived at his widow's home, which was up a dusty, rocky, and hilly road. My security detail advised me that it would be best if we parked the car and walked up the hill to meet the family. They were concerned our armored vehicle would have difficulty making it up the final stretch, and they didn't want it to get stuck. So, the safest way to get to the house was to walk the final stretch.

As I walked to the widow's house, my security detail was spread out around me in every direction. We were armed with our weapons, armored vests, and tactical gear. I kicked up a cloud of red dirt and dust with every step because the ground was so dry. The only sound I heard was the occasional static coming from our radios. We walked in silence, and I looked carefully in every direction. I could hear loud noises in the distance and the occasional whistle of bullets as they flew by on my right side.

I must admit, I tried to be cool and act like I wasn't scared, but on the inside, I was nervous. I had been in high threat situations before, and I knew what to do from my training, but this was different. I felt very exposed walking through an open area with no buildings to serve as cover. I got that familiar knot in my stomach, and I tried to relax myself by taking deep breaths.

I walked into the widow's home escorted by an interpreter who guided me on the correct protocol and traditions to observe. I sat on the dirt-covered floor and breathed in the smell from the mud walls while the sons went in the back room and brought their mother out to meet me.

What an honor it was to have this family open their home to me and for me to be able to express my gratitude for their father and husband and all he did in service to the USA. I thought to myself, *This is another once-in-a-lifetime opportunity*, as I stayed and had a cup of hot tea with a family I would never meet again.

The visit to the widow's home was a defining moment for me and helped shape the rest of my tour. It was a lesson in honoring local customs, and at a gut level, I was struck seeing firsthand the austere living conditions of the locals, not only in this home but on the drive to and from meeting the family. They were way tougher than I was.

Live as a leader and show up. Whether I was on a plane toe to toe with colleagues or working out of a repurposed bathroom, quickly restocking essential supplies, or sitting and quietly observing traditions, I had chance after chance to just show up and practice leadership in every new setting. I had to trust my team, both the ones working directly with me and those working back home at Langley.

One of my favorite books is called *True North: Discover Your Authentic Leadership* by Bill George. Bill's a senior fellow at Harvard and former CEO of Medtronic, and he teaches "You lead from where you are. You don't have to look for that next promotion. Wherever you are, you have that opportunity to step up and lead right now" (George and Sims 2007).

Leadership is *not just a title*—leadership is a way of *living, being, and interacting* with others in everyday life. Leaders can't do it alone; it takes teamwork.

CHAPTER 10

Being on the Team (Denver: 2021)

——

I love the arts, theater, opera, and symphony. Any live performance, and I'm there.

I also love an occasion to dress up and wear fancy clothes. Close friends invited me to the Opera Colorado Gala, and little did I know I would be sitting next to Cleo Parker Robinson. Cleo is an icon in the Denver art scene. She's a marvelous, genuine, and talented African American woman who received a Kennedy Center Medal of Honor and is known worldwide for her Denver-based dance troupe of over fifty years.

The purpose of the gala was to raise funds for Opera Colorado, and one of the auction items was the opportunity to be an extra in an upcoming opera, *Tosca*. No singing is required when you are an extra.

Cleo Parker Robinson, dressed in a dazzling red gown, reached over to me as the auctioneer started the bidding for the chance to be an extra in *Tosca*. Cleo whispered, "Darling, you must do this." And she raised her arm holding my bidder number—the number 184—high in the air to place *my* bid.

I asked, "Cleo, what are you doing?"

She responded, "Yes, darling, this is something you *must* do."

You'd think after saying yes to flying to the other side of the world into a war zone for an unknown amount of time that this would be easy, but it wasn't. I had to gather all my courage to say yes. I thought, *I have no business being in an opera*, then the word came out of my mouth, "*Yes.*"

The bidding went on, and the cost went up… but I thought, *If Cleo thinks this is important, then I must say yes.* I won the bid with a few others to join in.

But then Covid happened, the 2020 opera season was canceled, and I thought my opportunity to be an extra was gone. Part of me was relieved, but then I received an email that Opera Colorado was preparing for their first live opera performance in twenty months, and they wanted to know if I still wanted to participate. I thought, *Why not?* and again I said, "yes."

The experience began with my costume fitting. I drove to Opera Colorado's warehouse in an industrial park in North Denver. Three women pulled out a tape measure, took my measurements, asked if I preferred knee highs or full-length hose, and texted the opera director to see if I should have long or short sleeves on my dress. I was just an extra. I marveled at the professionalism and courtesy the wardrobe staff extended to me.

Then came the rehearsal schedule. I've known commitment in my day, and this was quite a commitment. Rehearsals were on the weekends and evenings. It's one thing to say yes and another to put in the work. But I was all in. This was going to be an opportunity to learn and experience something very new.

The rehearsal schedule had us in different locations from South Denver to the Studio Loft above the Ellie Caulkins Opera House in downtown Denver. Three full weeks of rehearsals culminated with the first on-stage rehearsal taking place at the Ellie Caulkins Opera House.

I stepped onto the stage, and I was in an 1800s Basilica in Rome. It was electrifying. I was nervous at every rehearsal, even though my role was simple. All I had to do was walk across the stage with my partner as if we were going to church. I thought, *What do I know about the opera?* If this had been about sneaking in communications gear or restocking critical supplies, I would have been in my element, but I had never been trained to act. Then came our first dress rehearsal.

My custom-fitted costume was a beautiful peach silk dress with lace, white shoes, and white hose. It was waiting for me in the dressing room. I was instructed to go downstairs to have my wig and bonnet put on by a wig expert who had worked with Opera Colorado for twenty years. Sarah put my hair in pin curls, on came the wig cap, then my beautiful wig. And then an eighteenth century bonnet. The bonnet was quite heavy and reminded me of wearing night vision goggles in Afghanistan. I enjoyed every minute of this new experience.

The wig experts played an important part in the overall opera production. As did many other experts, such as wardrobe, stage handlers, lighting, and orchestra. Opera is a full-on team effort.

I watched and observed. These were true professionals.

Everyone from the maestro to the choir director, principal singers to the adult and children's choirs to the woman who gave out parking passes had a vital role to play. I loved watching how it all came together. It was an example of teamwork at its finest. This team didn't have lives on the line, and they weren't saving hostages, but the stagehands, actors, and musicians worked together as tightly and professionally as if they were.

Three full weeks of rehearsals and it was opening night. Costume and wig on, I waited patiently in the green room, just off the stage. I watched singers move on and off the stage and the principals go through multiple costume changes. I listened carefully for the call, "Te Deum procession stage left." As I took a deep breath, I walked out on stage.

The opera house was filled with adoring crowds. The moment Ms. Citro came out of her dressing room, she said, "Ladies, let's have some fun tonight." Within two minutes, she was singing at incredible octaves that were enough to crack glass. She showed us that humility is important in all things, not just singing.

I saw this happen consistently with the other principal singers who congratulated, encouraged and were kind to everyone they interacted with.

The singers didn't have the title of chief of support, chief of station, or EXDIR, but they were leaders in every moment throughout the practices and performances. In every interaction, they set the tone and represented not just themselves but the art of opera. Just like when leaders from the CIA sat with the widows and drank tea, we were representing our agency, our military, and even our country.

Opening night of *Tosca* was an emotional ride for everyone. People waited twenty long months for the arts to return to Denver. The audience even gave a standing ovation before the start of Act 3.

It was a first for the Ellie Caulkins Opera House. Management acknowledged every member of the team during the curtain call, many who hadn't had a paycheck in almost two years. I got to be a part of it because I said yes.

I will always remember the burst of energy and electrifying sensation that went through me at the first rehearsal and stayed with me to the final curtain call. The *Tosca* experience gave me courage to continue to say yes and seek opportunities to be on other high-performing teams, even where I am a beginner.

PART 4

GOOD LEADERS DON'T JUST LEAD AT WORK

CHAPTER 11

Leading with Humility (Virginia: 1983)

———

A good swimmer doesn't always make a good swim coach.

It was 1983, and I had just graduated from Penn State. I missed swimming and wanted to stay connected to the sport. I learned that Fairfax County Park Authority (FCPA) was hiring an assistant coach for their Masters Swim Team. Masters swimming is organized swimming for adults. But at twenty-two years old, I was at least twenty years younger than all the swimmers on the team.

When I was in high school, my swim coach insisted that to train other swimmers, I had to learn how to coach. She explained that just because I was a good swimmer didn't mean I knew how to instruct others, so she taught me. I was hired to coach two of Northern Virginia Swim Leagues' (NVSL) summer teams, Hamlet and Tuckahoe. Coaching accommodated my workout schedule, and I enjoyed the step up in pay from my first job as a janitor.

I loved watching the kids get stronger and faster in the pool and being involved in competitive and spirited meets. Summer swim leagues are full of fun activities, such as pep rallies before big meets and all-you-can-eat crab leg meals at the Chesapeake Bay Seafood House or splurging at Farrell's Ice Cream Parlour to celebrate a big win. Swimmers know how to have fun.

I realized the FCPA coaching job would be a good opportunity to stay engaged in something I enjoyed as I waited for my security clearances to come through to work at the Agency. While the FCPA coaching position wasn't full time, it would provide some income while I waited.

This was my first experience teaching people older than me. In many ways, it was low stakes, and there wasn't much to lose, but I wanted to help the swimmers achieve their goals.

When I showed up, I wondered how they would respond to a "young kid" training them. I knew I had to show them I could coach, not tell them I could. While I was confident in my abilities, I knew it would take some tact to establish myself and gain their trust.

I approached the situation with humility and confidence. I let the swimmers know I was capable and yet I didn't want to be boastful about my success as a swimmer. I also knew it was important to develop my relationship with the established head coach, Frank, and I knew it would take time to develop the trust that is essential in any coach/athlete relationship. I showed up at each practice with enthusiasm and a genuine desire to make the swimmers the best they could be.

It turned out my relationship with the swimmers and the head coach grew strong, and many of the swimmers went on to compete at the national level and were successful in various open water swims. There were others content to swim for fitness and found enjoyment in the social aspects of the team.

I had a great experience coaching the FCPA team until I moved abroad for my first overseas assignment. Little did I know at the time what a useful training ground this would be for some of the dynamics I would face as a young leader at the Agency. We find opportunities in unexpected places.

I was hired into the Agency's Supply Officer Trainee (SOT) program in 1983, a new program that included a surge in hiring women into logistics. The program was designed to provide training and assignments to accelerate our learning, prepare us for overseas positions, and develop the future leaders of logistics.

When I arrived, I was presented with a detailed training plan for the next twelve months. My schedule included working in various departments, such as small procurements, cataloging and inventory management, trucking and transportation, warehouse operations, and accountable property.

I was integrated with the staff of each department for hands-on training. Supervisors explained the intricacies of their area of responsibility. "Katy, you have to annotate a secure method of shipping when you submit a procurement and shipping request." I was given small projects to work on, such as inventorying accountable property and cataloging equipment. When the supervisors knew I was ready, they moved me into more complex tasks. They were the ones who ultimately prepared me to move into my first assignment in the foreign field.

I was part of this new cadre, and we were expected to "go anywhere, anytime." Mobility was the differentiator between SOTs and headquarters (HQS) based logistics officers. SOT promotions weren't guaranteed, but success overseas, a can-do attitude, and a willingness to take positions of increased responsibility led to steady promotions as a junior logs officer. We were also given "stretch assignments," and as a result, my first few promotions came more quickly compared to my HQS-based colleagues.

This caused friction with some of the officers who had been around longer, especially when I was promoted to a higher level on the general service (GS) pay scale. As I stood at the microwave heating my lunch one day, I overheard a conversation between some of my trainers. "Why is she getting promoted so quickly? We are the ones training her." It made me uneasy, and I wasn't sure how to broach the subject. I said nothing.

I knew I was on a faster track than others who thought their promotions should come at the same pace. It was hard for some officers to accept the new system. I understood their concerns, and I also knew the SOT track was created to ensure the Agency had logistics officers willing to serve in field positions. It was a new system, and it would take time for everyone to adjust.

I was self-conscious when I was promoted to levels beyond the people who trained me. Each time I was promoted, I graciously accepted my certificate and quietly went on with my work. I didn't want to appear boastful and upset my elders in the workplace.

This uneasy feeling also happened when I went into my first HQS supervisory position. I was in my twenties and supervising a branch with people in their forties and fifties. That was when I started to explore different leadership styles to see what worked.

I tried a directive leadership style, but that didn't work well for me. I tried treating everyone the same no matter how they behaved. That wasn't effective either. Eventually, I realized I was most effective when I adapted my approach depending on the employee. I had to be consistent with some things, such as coming to work on time, reporting attendance correctly, and doing one's job. However, employees were motivated by different things. I tried to understand what was most important to an employee and lead them with that in mind. Flexibility and adaptability were key.

My influence came from me, not from the position I held. Meeting the mission and getting the job done were important, but people were more willing to focus on work and the mission when I showed interest in them as a person.

That's what motivated me too. I was busy in my office one day when the director of logistics walked through my work area with his hand raised over his head waving a *Washington Post* article. His office was in another building, so it was unusual for him to be in our space. We didn't know why he was there, but it turned out he was looking for me. "Where is Katy McQuaid? Where is the woman who swam under the bridge most of us are afraid to drive over?"

I was a top female finisher in the Great Chesapeake Bay 4.4-mile Swim the weekend before. In addition to the newspaper article, he brought me a handwritten card: "Katy, congratulations on your top finish in the Chesapeake Bay Swim. The Agency is lucky to have you." I was embarrassed, and yet the impact of his gesture was very powerful. I couldn't believe a senior leader noticed my swim across the water that passes under the Bay Bridge and that he took the time to recognize me. It left me with the impression that he cared. In that moment, I knew I wanted to do that for others.

His actions inspired me to get to know my staff better. I started to ask people questions, be curious, and find out what was important to them. In turn, trust began to build, and people were happier, which ultimately led to a higher performing team. This is when I began to learn how to lead with humility and confidence.

CHAPTER 12

Ripple Effect
(USA: 1997, 2009)

———

There's this thing that happens when you work with classified material, secrets, *and* you cannot tell people where you work.

Life as an Agency officer extends beyond the workplace, especially when you're stationed overseas. In addition to working in the office during the day resolving logistical issues—evenings and weekends were filled with "official events." Colleagues were often neighbors and families whose children went to the same schools. I learned quickly the impact of my everyday leadership decisions went beyond the individual employee I was working with.

I wasn't just leading the people who directly reported to me. Every decision I made not only impacted the person I was working with, but it impacted their spouse, their children, their children's teachers, coaches, neighbors, and their community.

I knew the impact on me of decisions made by my leaders. Sometimes those decisions had a positive effect, and other times, not so much. There were nights I just kept replaying the events of the day in my head. I used to hear "don't bring home into the office with you," but I took the office home with me more than I care to admit.

I faced every leadership decision I made knowing this was about more than the employee. And, while it was important to consider the lives I was impacting, in retrospect, I internalized a lot of stress regarding some of these decisions. When I was the chief of base at a facility, there was an employee, with a wife and three young children, who was assigned there. I grew to know this employee's family over time, and a few things concerned me. Jack's wife had difficulty fitting in and often mentioned having challenges at home. They would come by my house occasionally to visit my Bengal cat, Venus. The kids thought she looked like a cheetah. That's when I noticed their nine-year-old son didn't speak in complete sentences even though he attended school with all the other children.

Jack was selected to fill a position in Asia, in a city that had a very high rate of terrorism, crime, pollution, traffic, and crowded living conditions. I'd traveled there and knew it would be a difficult assignment for the family.

I sensed their tour would be filled with issues and likely end in a shortened tour. When a shortened tour occurs, it is hard on the family, costly for everyone involved, and disruptive for the organization. But more so, I was concerned for Jack's family than the Agency.

The Agency has a clearance process for employees and their families. A clearance is required prior to finalizing an overseas assignment. I was hopeful that during the clearance process, the son's delayed speech would be identified and he would get the attention he needed.

The family lived on base in government housing, and they were going through the checkout process, their assignment to Asia on track. I was sitting at my desk one morning when two employees came into my office and their faces were white as sheets. One of them was so disturbed she was shaking. "You've got to do something."

They found Jack's home in derelict condition on the pre-move inspection. Trash, feces, diapers, weeks of dirty dishes were in the kitchen sink, and belongings strewn everywhere. The facilities employees feared for the welfare of the children living in those conditions. They pleaded, "Katy, please, you've got to call Child Protective Services."

I immediately engaged the Agency's office of medical services to dispatch a psychologist to meet with the family and assess the situation. I wanted the family to get the care, support, and attention they needed. I also wanted to make sure they weren't going to be put into harm's way if they went to Asia.

Ultimately, the family's assignment was canceled, and they were transferred back to Langley for Jack's next assignment, and appropriate medical care was provided.

The family was still living on base before their departure when I pulled up in my car to the community mailboxes at the end of the street. Jack's wife drove in behind me, and I thought, *Oh boy, she's going to be really upset with me. I need to be prepared.* I stepped out of my car as she got out of hers, bracing myself for an angry woman.

"Katy, I just want to thank you. I am so grateful you said something because now I can get the help I know we need." She kept saying, "Thank you, I am so grateful."

She explained that she wanted to get help for her family but had been keeping it all in for years because her husband asked her to keep quiet. Jack didn't want her to jeopardize a potential overseas assignment.

She said, "I have hope for the first time in years, and I don't have to hide anymore." She went on to explain that she was looking forward to getting counseling and treatment for the family.

In that moment, tears welled up in my eyes. I regretted that I hadn't acted sooner when I sensed something was wrong. I wished I had been more courageous and gotten her help already. It had a profound effect on me to see the ripple effect. The ripple effect ended up serving the greater good.

SERVING THE GREATER GOOD

I overheard my dad talking on the phone while I stood at the top of the stairs when I was nine years old. He was having a conversation with his brother, and they were talking about money. My uncle Ronnie needed money for something. When my dad hung up the phone, I said, "Dad, I'd like to help Uncle Ronnie." I pulled the coins out of my piggy bank. "Here's the money I've saved up." He responded, "Katy, it is nice of you to offer to help, but I want you to keep your money, and I want you to know your uncle will be fine."

I don't know why, but even as a child, I cared about other people, and I often put their needs before mine. My "go to" is to think about the other person, team, organization, or group I'm involved with. I call it serving the greater good; it is my purpose. I think I was born that way or just wired that way. I was always looking out for the kid who was sitting alone in the school cafeteria or was the last one picked for the team in gym class. That's a lonely feeling, and I didn't want anyone to feel excluded.

That's why I loved the position I was asked to fill when I came back from a three-year tour in Asia. I was assigned as chief of employee development for hundreds of CIA logistics officers. It was a position I'd always dreamed about but never thought I'd get. The position was normally filled by a GS-15, someone who was an "up and comer" in the career service. I didn't see myself as an "up and comer," and I was only a GS-14 at the time.

The logistics' chief of employee development was responsible for hiring, training, assignments, promotion panels, and assisted with disciplinary actions. It was a dream job for me because I always wanted to be involved with the human resources side of the organization—building strong work units and creating growth opportunities for individuals' careers. I'd always been fascinated by human behavior and team dynamics. What really makes people tick and what motivates them? Who can we put together to make a really strong team to meet the mission?

Back then, we didn't interview for a new position in the CIA; we were assigned to a new job every two to three years by the employee development staff. The process certainly wasn't a perfect art; it was more like sausage making. When making assignments, the employee development officers (EDOs) took into consideration meeting the needs of the mission while trying to balance "stretch" opportunities for officers, building diverse teams, and blending talent. At times, we had to make accommodations for an employee to address personal needs.

There were many opportunities for me to serve the greater good in this position.

The CIA requires a security clearance and a full scope polygraph—also called lie detector test—for applicants to be hired. A trained examiner administers the polygraph exam periodically throughout an employee's career. A full scope poly requires one to be hooked up to a machine with four to six wires attached to sensors and a belt wrapped around the chest—just like you see in the movies. The sensors measure the breathing rate, pulse, blood pressure, and perspiration to detect if someone is lying.

While the polygraph exam doesn't hurt, it is not fun. I found the experience demeaning every time I had one. I didn't have anything to hide, and even though it was part of the process, I wanted the Agency to trust me. I was always nervous when an exam started. I could hear my heartbeat pulsing in my ears.

I didn't like being strapped to a machine while I stared at a wall. I knew I was being observed even when the polygrapher stepped out of the room. It helped me to take slow and deep breaths to calm my nervous system. I silently counted, "One, two, three, four... hold... exhale, two, three, four."

I'd think, *How many of my friends would put up with this?* My first polygraph—also known as the entrance on duty poly— was the most uncomfortable and took four hours. My last polygraph took no more than fifteen minutes from start to finish. That was a relief.

A security clearance isn't 100 percent failsafe—the goal is to hire people who aren't susceptible to blackmail. The polygraph is used to assess a person's financial stability, lifestyle, use of technology, and one's ability to keep classified information within proper channels. Security clearances are updated periodically through one's career.

The employee development process looked simple from the outside, but it wasn't. It was the first time in my career when I could see the information managers had to work with behind the scenes. "This officer" was unable to take certain positions because they were in severe financial debt. "This officer" was in the process of a divorce and couldn't take a position overseas because of child custody issues. "This officer" had a child with special needs and needed to be assigned to a country with adequate schooling for their child. All the while trying to make sure we had the right talent in the right country and the right amount of career development opportunities for the officer. It was like putting together a 2000-piece floral jigsaw puzzle, except this was people's lives.

We also had to ensure the CIA could meet its mission to bring human intelligence back to the US president and policymakers so we could protect and keep America safe.

Never once did I assign an officer to a position and not consider the impact on them and the ripple effect it would have on their family, their friends, and their long-term career development. In my mind came the question, what serves the greater good?

There was an amazing officer who was selected to fill a coveted position in Europe. The position was exactly what I wanted at the start of my career. I asked him to come to my office so I could inform him he was being assigned to this highly sought-after position. Everyone wanted to go there. I thought, *This is going to be an easy meeting. Certainly Tom will be pleased to hear he is going to Europe.*

Tom came into my office, and I started the conversation. "I have some good news for you."

Then I noticed Tom kept standing and wouldn't sit down in the chair across from my desk. I knew something was up. He looked me straight in the eyes and said, "Katy, I can't go to Europe." Tom closed the door so no one would hear what he was about to tell me. He said he didn't want people to know, but his wife had ALS and the disease had progressed to the point she was in a wheelchair. He said, "I can't go to Europe because we need to be in Virginia to be close to my wife's medical care."

In that very moment, all I could think about, care about, was Tom and his family. I would find someone else to go to Europe, and the mission would be met. But what about Tom?

Instead of going to Europe, Tom was assigned to a position where he led the logistics officer training branch. An important position where he influenced logistics officers training and development.

Five years later, I was the deputy director of logistics, and Tom set up a time to meet with me. When he came into my office, he wouldn't sit down. I wasn't prepared for what he was about to say as he stood in my office.

"Katy, I just can't keep it up. It's gotten to be too much. I must resign because I need to be close to home in case of an emergency." I couldn't believe what I had heard, so I asked him, "Did you really say you are going to resign?"

He said yes as he shook his head from side to side. Tom explained his wife's ALS had progressed to a point that she couldn't be at home alone, and if the care provider didn't show up, he needed to get home immediately from work. Tom shared with me some very difficult moments that had recently happened when the care provider didn't show up and he didn't get the message in a timely manner.

I must explain, Tom was an extremely talented officer, and the CIA had invested heavily in him with his security clearance and training. Most importantly, I didn't want to lose Tom because he was one of our top logistics officers and a mentor and leader to the officers who worked with him.

He was smart, analytical, an amazing communicator with a can-do attitude. He was the type of employee we *did not* want to lose, but what could I do?

I came up with a solution one day as I visited one of our bases. While I was on my tour of the base, the employees insisted I needed to see the housing area because the homes were new. As I walked through the first one, I realized the houses were perfect for Tom's situation. The homes were ranch style, wheelchair accessible, *and* they were less than a mile from the office. There was a position opening within the year, and it would provide Tom with an opportunity to build new skills. It would be great for his career progression, and we could accommodate his family's special needs.

I couldn't wait to get back to Langley, and as soon as I arrived, I asked Tom to come see me. It's funny but, this time when he came in, he sat down in the chair in my office. I guess it was his turn to know something was up.

"Tom, I think I've found a win-win for your situation." He looked at me with tears in his eyes and said, "You know, Katy, no one in my career has cared about me as much as you do."

That was eighteen years ago, and because I was looking out for the greater good, Tom recently retired after a distinguished forty-year career in the CIA.

Both Tom's and Jack's stories were reminders that every single leadership decision I made impacted not only the employees but their families. Those leadership decisions also impacted the organization. Adversity is real, and it takes a strong organization to help people get through those times. When members are supported through times of adversity, it strengthens the organization and builds trust. There is a delicate balance between running operations and being responsible for the well-being of the employees and their families, but organizations are only as strong as their weakest link.

CHAPTER 13

Allowing
Others to Shine
(Afghanistan: 2006)

One of the best leaders I worked with was my chief of station (COS) in Afghanistan. He was a great mentor and leader. The COS is a very powerful position in CIA hierarchy. They are responsible for all Agency operations in a country, and they make the go/no go decision for all station activities. "Chief" was my COS in the conflict zone, and he really cared about the people he worked with.

He walked the walk and talked the talk. His everyday interactions were proof of this.

Chief was extremely driven when it came to keeping America safe. He maintained personal humility with an intense professional will. One of the things I truly admired was his ability to quickly see the big picture and figure out what needed to be done. He was strategic and tactical at the same time. As important as a mission was, he constantly looked out for officers and helped them succeed. He had an endearing way of calling everyone Chief.

Upon learning of my assignment as chief of support in Afghanistan, I wrote Chief an email to let him know I was looking forward to working for him. He responded, "Katy, you will be working with me, not for me."

The days were long as we typically worked seven days a week from 7:30 a.m. to 10:00 p.m. Yes, we'd take breaks during the day, but those were for meals or to get in a workout. For the most part, we were always on the clock except to sleep or call home.

I often stayed in my office late at night to catch up with my colleagues in Langley. Because of the time difference, they were just starting their day when it was dinner time for me.

Chief would pass by my office on the way to his hooch for the night. "Katy, I keep telling you, this is a marathon, not a sprint. Time to call it a night."

The support team kept a freezer well stocked with candy they received in care packages from home because they knew Chief loved chocolate. On his way to his hooch, Chief would grab a handful of M&M's from the freezer and comment, "I love my support team."

I think it also says a lot about Chief that half of the station's leadership positions were filled by women. A station this size would typically have no more than one or two women in key leadership positions. Chief placed value in an officer's work ethic, talent, and willingness to be held accountable. He hired people with these attributes; their gender didn't matter.

Chief took the time to know the people on his team and learn what mattered the most to them. He understood one of my favorite pastimes was watching Penn State football.

I was in the office the morning of January 3, and Chief came up to me and said, "Katy, it's time for you to go back to your hooch."

I looked at him with concern and said, "Why, what's going on?"

"Penn State is playing in the Orange Bowl, and it's more important for you to watch the game than it is for you to be in the office."

I insisted it wasn't necessary to watch the game, and he insisted it was. Guess who won that argument. Not me.

As I walked back to my hooch to watch the game, I was on top of the world. I was happy I was going to watch Penn State play football, but I was even happier knowing I had a boss who cared about me. Such a simple act of leadership meant so much.

Two years in Afghanistan, and Chief's assignment was ending. He was getting ready to leave the country and wanted me to be at his farewell dinner. He casually walked into my office. "Katy, President Karzai is having a farewell dinner for me next week, and I'd like you to be there."

My first response was "No, surely you don't need me there, and I don't have the right clothes."

But Chief insisted.

A few days later, we split up into different vehicles with our security details and went to the Afghan presidential palace. When we arrived, President Karzai was in the middle of an interview with the BBC, so we sat in the garden enjoying a slight breeze and sipped fresh-squeezed orange juice while we waited.

When President Karzai approached, he embraced Chief and, with a big smile on his face, said, "Chief, you are a very good man. I am going to miss you."

Six of us who were part of Chief's leadership team walked into Karzai's office as he invited us to sit in finely upholstered blue and gold fabric chairs. We were positioned in a semi-circle close to the president, who sat on an ornately carved high-back chair with red velvet cushions. Karzai looked at each one of us and told the story of meeting Chief and then he went on to share highlights of their yearslong working relationship. I was captivated as I listened intently to each story that conveyed the risk, bravery, dedication, and selfless nature of Chief.

The president signaled to one of his aides, who brought over a six-inch square dark wooden box with a gold emblem on it.

As he opened it, Karzai pulled out a large bronze medal and read a citation recognizing Chief with the highest civilian honor in the country. I choked back tears as I watched Chief accept his well-deserved award.

After the medal presentation, we went to the president's residence for dinner. We walked into the dining room, where the president's men were already waiting. I went toward the seat at the end of a very long ornately carved dining table. This was one of my shy moments, and I was trying to stay under the radar and sit as far away from President Karzai and Chief as possible. It made sense to me to have those with more "operational" positions sit closer to the VIPs.

All of a sudden, I heard, "Katy, you sit here," and President Karzai pointed to the seat next to him. I was surprised, and I blushed. I replied, "No, I'll just sit here; that is where Chief needs to sit." Karzai then said, "No, it's where you will sit... Chief can sit on the other side of me." It was another one of those times I knew to be quiet, and I sat next to President Karzai.

We had an amazing traditional Afghan meal that was beautifully prepared. I lost count of how many dishes were brought to the table, but each entrée that came out was delicious. President Karzai leaned over to me and quietly shared, "The kebab goes with the green rice; the cooked vegetables must be eaten with the yellow rice."

He shared information about each dish, the significance of it, and what sauce went with what protein. At one point, President Karzai grabbed my arm, and the whole table paused. "Don't eat that dish. I'm afraid you'll get sick from the uncooked tomatoes."

As Karzai took care of me through the meal, I could see Chief just smile and look at me as if to say, "Atta girl, this is where you belong."

There were times I didn't get things right or there were issues that needed my immediate attention. Chief didn't hesitate to call me into his office and let me know what needed to be done. No matter the intensity of the circumstances, he remained calm and communicated effectively. I learned from each situation because he gracefully advised and corrected in a way that served to coach me and support the mission.

I was motivated when my boss understood my values and what was important to me. That's the type of leader I wanted to work with—someone who truly cared about the individuals on their team and someone who brought out the best in people.

A team's success reflects you and how well you have led them. When a team member advances or is promoted into a new position off your team, it's a win-win, even if that means they all progress and move into new positions and teams of which you are not the leader. When your team shines, you do as well.

CHAPTER 14

A Day in the Life (Persian Gulf: 1991)

———

At the age of twenty-two, I was working for the CIA, and I was learning a lot. I worked there for thirty-two years, and amongst the many lessons I learned, there were three that stood out: just say yes, the value of teamwork, and that leadership is a way of life.

One day, I was sitting at my desk at CIA HQS in Virginia when I got a call on the green line. Back in those days, secure phones were green and sat on our desks, and there was no caller ID. I picked up the receiver and heard the voice of one of my *big* bosses.

"Katy, we know the Gulf War is going to start in four days, and we need a logistics officer with your field experience to go over there to support a special project."

I had an immediate rush of adrenaline, and my heart began to race. I was excited by the opportunity and immediately said, "Sure, I'll go."

Then my boss said, "Wait, let me tell you a few things before you say yes. We need you to be on site in four days, we don't know how long you'll be gone, and you'll be the only woman working with a group of men who are special operations officers."

I replied, "I can do it. I grew up with four brothers. I will be fine."

Saying yes is a part of the culture in the CIA, and while I accepted it, it wasn't always easy. In this case, I said yes and knew I could do it, but I did worry about leaving my team. At the time, I was supervising the logistics branch in the CIA's University.

I worried about leaving without a transition plan for ongoing activities. Once I left for the Gulf War, I'd be leaving my team for good.

I didn't know a lot about the new assignment, most importantly, how long I would be gone. I didn't know any of the special ops officers I'd be working with or about the country I was going to, but I had faith, and I knew I could trust my previous overseas experience to guide me.

I remember sitting on the plane wearing a pink- and white-checkered sweater, exhausted from four days of non-stop activity preparing to leave. My body was aching, tired, and I could barely keep my eyes open. All I wanted to do was fall asleep, but my mind kept thinking, *What have you done?* It's one thing to say yes, but "Katy, you have no idea how long you'll be gone or how things are going to unfold with the operation."

A pit of nervous energy appeared in my stomach, as typically happens when I am excited about something. I wasn't sure if I was nervous or excited, but I knew the project was important to our national security, and I wanted to be a part of it, yet I was stepping into the unknown.

I arrived at the CIA base in the Middle East, where we worked from the basement of an old dark building. We started each day with a morning operations (ops) meeting to go over the plan for the day.

My job on this mission was to securely procure and ship the team's equipment to strategic locations around the country. The gear needed to be available for the team when the mission started, and we knew it would be soon. We were gearing up for a long road ahead.

My main challenges were learning a new environment and being the only logistics officer supporting the team. The stakes were high because a mistake could tank my career and because I didn't have a fellow logs officer to collaborate with.

I spent time with the team reviewing our ops plan and making sure our activities meshed with the overall Desert Storm effort. We reviewed our contingency plans and adjusted as necessary.

I enjoyed the daily morning meetings with my teammates because we ate pistachio nuts and drank coffee for breakfast. Sometimes we challenged each other to see who had the largest pile of pistachio shells by the end of the meeting.

I stayed in the InterContinental Hotel because the boss didn't want me to share living facilities with the guys. They stayed in an apartment on the edge of town, and I walked to and from work each day by myself. I was hyper-vigilant and on the lookout for someone out of place or following me too closely. I was aware of bomb threats in the area, and I always had my guard up.

I had spent two nights in the hotel when the boss came to me. "Katy, it is just too dangerous for you to stay in the hotel. You need to move to an apartment with the guys."

He was right. The facade of my hotel was mostly glass, which is very dangerous and made it a more likely target because Westerners were staying there.

At first, I thought, *Oh boy*, and then I realized I really didn't have a choice. I said, "I'll do it… as long as I have my own bedroom."

I must admit, there was a sense of relief when I was asked to move into the apartment. I no longer walked to work by myself, constantly looking around and surveilling the situation to be sure I was safe. Instead, I rode in the safety of a vehicle with my highly trained special ops officer teammates.

Teamwork is key, and I didn't realize when I said yes to staying in the apartment that one of my roommates—a former Army Ranger—would make lunch for me every day. As I came out of my room each morning, a brown bag was waiting for me on the counter with my lunch inside. Scott would then ask me, "Do you want one or two Little Debbie's with your lunch?" I love it when someone prepares a meal for me, so this was an unexpected benefit, and it showed that teamwork went beyond our official duties.

As quickly as our special operation started, it ended. The Allied Forces swiftly succeeded in Operation Desert Storm, which meant my teammates returned to Langley within weeks to prepare for their next mission. I remained in-country for a few months to close the warehouse operation and prepare the gear for secure transport back to the United States.

When I said yes to supporting the special project on four days' notice, I got the opportunity to learn a new country, a new culture, work on a cool special operation, and most importantly, I worked with an amazing team of people, some who became lifelong friends.

Some of my best experiences in life happened when I just said yes and leaned on people who were smarter than me. Whether I was flying in a helicopter in the dark of night or scuba diving in the South China Sea, I used my faith to guide me, and I knew it wouldn't steer me wrong.

PART 5

LEARN & LAUGH AT YOURSELF

CHAPTER 15

Vulnerability (Eurasia: 1991)

I never thought I had any major fears or phobias. None of the typical fears affected me—until one did. It happened to me when I least expected it.

One cold and drizzly February afternoon in Eurasia, a couple of my colleagues suggested we explore around the city. It was a rare day off, so I jumped at the opportunity. I didn't think anything of it. That is, until we visited a historic castle that dated to the Roman era. Made of white quartz stone, it sat on a tall mountain and was one of this capital city's oldest sites.

The thing I enjoy most about traveling is trying new foods and eating the local cuisine. I was interested in touring the castle, but I was more interested in finding a place to eat once we were done. I was excited to find a new restaurant in this part of town because I couldn't get enough of their special kebab. A dish of lamb cooked in spicy tomato sauce and butter melted on top, served over rice and pita bread with yogurt. Another favorite of mine was dolma, fragrant stuffed grape leaves that have a subtle spicy cinnamon and allspice aroma.

The guys and I arrived at the castle, and there weren't many people around, probably because the weather was cold and it wasn't tourist season. We toured the grounds before we went up the steps to get to the top of the castle and look out over the city. Our view was obscured by the dark, thick smoke that hovered above. The haze was from the coal locals burned to provide heat in the winter.

One of the guys suggested it was time to go, and we started to leave down the narrow staircase, which was on the outside of the building. I didn't notice it on the way up, but there wasn't a handrail, and the white quartz stones were polished from people walking on them for hundreds of years. They were *very* slippery. Suddenly, I felt a fear rush over me, and I started to sweat. Without a handrail, I could easily fall. The fear paralyzed me. I tried to make myself walk down the steps without saying anything, but my legs wouldn't move.

I was so used to toughing it out and muscling through situations, I didn't want to say anything to the guys. As if speaking up would mean I was weak, but I couldn't go on. I decided the only way I would get down to the ground was to basically crawl down the stairs. In that moment, I didn't care what the guys thought. So, I sat down and began to make my way using my bum, arms, and legs to guide me down the steps.

It was the first time in my life I remember being terrified, and the fear came out of nowhere. I was able to laugh about it when I was safely back on the ground. The guys laughed too as they teased me about being a ninja. Visiting the castle had been a lot of fun, so I didn't give it much thought until it happened again.

I was on a tour of a radome, a large white structure that looks like the biggest golf ball you've ever seen. Its purpose is to protect satellite dishes from the elements. The satellite dish is an important part of the intelligence mission because it receives data from satellites that are up in space.

I was with a small group of people, and we had to climb a lot of stairs to get to the top. The stairs were made of metal, and they made a pinging sound each time my foot landed on a step. The group climbed up for a while and then stopped at a landing. We continued to climb to the next landing and the next. When we made it to the top, I gazed down at the men and women working below us. It was so dizzying that I had to close my eyes at times. We were *way* up there.

The gentleman guiding the tour leaned against the railing as he shared information about the satellite dish. Suddenly, my heart started racing, I could hardly breathe, and I felt my face turn red. The guide was using his hands to point to various parts of the dish, and all I could think was he might fall over the railing, and it was a long way down to the ground.

I forced myself to take some deep belly breaths to calm my nerves. I used the handrails instead of my bum to get down the stairs this time. I was so happy when I finally reached the ground. I made a pledge to myself that I was never doing that again.

After this, I realized my experience in Eurasia wasn't a one off; I had a fear of heights. I had no idea how or why the fear started. When it shows up, I always think I can talk myself out of it or push through, but it doesn't seem to work that way. I try to rationalize with myself, and the only thing that seems to work is intentional deep breaths and getting down closer to the ground.

I learned fear can come up suddenly, but it doesn't make me weak. Fears are inevitable, and they don't make a person weak. Weakness is allowing that fear to stop you from living life fully.

What this newfound fear taught me was that it was okay to be vulnerable around others; it made me human. Allowing others to know I was afraid brought humor to each situation. From the guys kidding me about being a ninja to a woman on the radome tour who joked, "I thought I was the only one shaking in my boots standing on the top landing," laughter relieved some of the tension.

When fear arises and we acknowledge it, it has less power over us. It helps us understand our limitations and learn to adapt to them so we can prepare for the best ways to get through them the next time.

CHAPTER 16

Attitude Matters (Southeast Asia: 1994)

___

As a child, I would beg my parents to take me with them whenever they went to play a round of golf. They always said no, and I never played golf with them until I became an adult. I eventually realized playing golf was my parents' "date night." It was their opportunity for some alone time without any of us five kids intruding.

Golf always intrigued me, and my desire to play stayed with me, even though I was much better with water sports than land sports.

When I was stationed in Asia, there was a group of guys who played 18 holes of golf every Sunday at 5:00 a.m. Their trio included the CIA's chief of station (COS) and two other men from the office who were professional-level golfers. The guys knew I was interested in playing, so when they had an opening after the COS departed the country, they invited me to play with them.

My first reaction was to decline because I assumed they only wanted golfers of their caliber to play with them.

"I'm sure they don't know how much of a beginner I truly am."

One of the guys, Tony, was very clear with me. "Katy, we enjoy having you around, and we will help you learn to play golf. All you must do is pay attention and keep up. If you stay up with us, you will be fine." So, I said yes and decided to join them. I felt lucky to have the opportunity to play golf on a regular basis, and with pros.

The most difficult part of playing with the group was getting up early in the morning. I'm not a morning person. We teed off the first hole as the sun was just starting to rise. I did it because I wanted to learn to play golf, and I was learning from talented golfers. I was nervous the first few times I swung a club with them, but I eventually settled into it.

My contribution was adding self-deprecating humor to the mix. That was easy for me. I brought something to the group that was lacking; I was someone they could have fun with. I was serious about learning, and I was good at laughing at myself.

I was happy once I got into the rhythm of playing 18 holes in the humidity. The golf course had a mini restaurant offering food and drink at every hole. This slowed play down considerably. Along the way, I ate hard-boiled eggs with soy sauce or green noodles with coconut milk. The local food was a big part of the experience for me.

I played golf with them nearly every week for a couple of years. I must admit, my golf game got better, but I never got good. I could hit a mean tee shot, but my chipping and putting game was bad, and it's still bad. I can still hear Tony saying, "Put your hips into it, McQuaid."

I was sought after to be part of a foursome in Scramble tournaments. That's because I could hit a long tee shot and I had the advantage of starting from the women's tee, which means starting closer to the pin. In Scramble tournaments, each team uses the best shot of the four players. That's about all I was good for, in addition to providing laughs. I was a "one shot wonder," and the guys knew the only shot they could count on was my first shot from the women's tee. But this made me a valuable teammate!

I knew I was never going to be a stellar golfer, not even close. I set out to learn and experience something new, and I was open to playing a sport where I wasn't as good as the others. I played golf because I wanted to learn, have fun, and get to know my colleagues better. I showed up each Sunday with sunscreen on and a good attitude, and I was receptive to coaching. That's why the guys included me week after week. The experience taught me that if I stayed focused and kept a good attitude, my skill level didn't matter.

CHAPTER 17

Laughing at One's Self (Afghanistan: 2005)

A life lived abroad requires the creation of new traditions around the holidays. New traditions don't replace the ones I grew up with, like eating lasagna and opening one present on Christmas Eve.

One of the most memorable holiday parties I attended was in Kabul, Afghanistan. The office celebrated the holidays with a white elephant gift exchange. It was a popular Christmas event where amusing or impractical gifts were exchanged, and people vied to walk away with the best present. The goal was to entertain and garner laughs rather than to gain a valuable gift, although that could happen.

We worked seven days a week in the conflict zone, and it wasn't often we took time to celebrate. It was easy to get caught up in the daily stresses of working in an unsafe environment and the high tempo of work requirements. Chief reminded us we needed to take a little downtime. It was a good way for the team to enjoy each other's company and share a few laughs. The annual holiday party was one of those times.

Signs went up in the hallways encouraging everyone to attend the party. The invite mentioned a special dinner to be served, followed by the white elephant gift exchange. The party arrangers even set up a Christmas tree with lights in the dining hall. The air was filled with excitement.

Finding a unique gift wasn't easy, and creativity was required. That's because I didn't have a junk drawer or closet filled with things just waiting to be regifted, like a scented candle or journal I received for my birthday. So, I looked around my hooch to see what I could find. I ended up gifting bottles of shampoo and conditioner.

Everyone received a numbered ticket as they entered the dining hall, and it determined the order for picking a gift, which were gathered in a pile on a table. Participants went in numerical order, and we were allowed to pick a gift from the pile or take a gift that someone else already opened. A gift could only be "stolen" two times after the initial opening.

When the first person picked their gift from the table, everyone ooh'd and ahh'd. Number two followed suit and then number three picked a large package wrapped in brown paper.

The package was three feet wide and four feet high and appeared light weight. When the lucky winner opened it, the room busted out in laughter. Inside was a painting from one of the older kids at an orphanage outside of Kabul. Our office supported the orphanage with regular visits, and one way we supported them was to buy their paintings.

This painting looked like Jesus with a red X across his face. I thought, *Why is everyone laughing about a portrait of Jesus with a red X?* It wasn't a masterpiece, and I thought it was irreverent. I didn't see the humor in it, and it didn't make sense to me.

The person with number four "stole" the painting from the number three person. Again, the room roared with laughter. I still couldn't figure out what was so funny. The following person grabbed a gift from the table, but right after him, the next person "stole" the painting for the second time.

There was banter between the person giving up the painting and the new "owner." It was fun to be in a room with everyone laughing, even if I didn't get the joke. I was slow on the uptake on this one.

Then it dawned on me. The reason everybody thought the painting was hilarious is that it was a painting of Osama bin Laden, not Jesus. I finally got the joke.

That night was special for me because it was so much fun. It reminded me of the importance of taking a break and enjoying my colleagues' company. It also helped me see the fun side of others and how important it is to laugh at myself.

I was mid-career before I understood the importance of showing my authentic self, a person who was willing to laugh at their mistakes. I also underestimated the value of informal office parties. For years, I was so focused on the mission, I missed opportunities to lead more effectively. I didn't make time for "non-essential" events like a chili cook-off or an end-of-fiscal- year celebration because I didn't want to extend my day.

As I moved into positions with increased responsibility, I realized an important part of leadership was to attend these events. I love to laugh, and I enjoy it the most when I'm laughing at myself. I didn't always have to be so serious and professional. It was a better reflection of the true me when I began to engage authentically. It also helped others realize we are all human and we all make mistakes, so it's okay for them to make some too.

PART 6

HUMBLE YET FIERCE

CHAPTER 18

Humility in Shining Moments (New York and Pennsylvania 1971–1980)

———

I grew up on Grand Island, New York. To keep us busy and out of trouble, my parents put us on a swim team. My brothers and I swam with the Water Buffalos, and our team colors were blue and gold.

We were in a dual meet against our rivals, and the meet was held in an old six-lane pool with dingy yellow walls, a diving board at one end, and the air filled with the thick smell of chlorine. The meet came down to the final event; the winner of my girl's relay would determine the winner of the meet.

The air hummed with anticipation. The starter fired his pistol into the air, and the relay was off. A relay consists of four swimmers, and I was the relay anchor, which meant I was the last one to swim. I was laser focused, waiting for the person swimming the third leg to touch the wall so I could get started. When my teammate touched the wall, we were a couple of body lengths behind the other team. Parents and swimmers were yelling at the top of their lungs; the cheering was super loud. "Come on, you've got it, go, go, go!" I didn't want to let my team down; my adrenaline was flowing.

In addition to being a strong swimmer, I loved a challenge, and it's safe to say I had a fierce competitive streak.

As I dove in the pool, I gave it my all. I kept my head down and pulled my arms through the water. My arms tingled because I held back on my breathing as I pushed harder. The water swished by my ears as I started to catch up to the other team's swimmer. I caught up with her after I made the turn, and as I swam, my heart was pounding for the last twenty-five yards. When I touched the wall, the whole room erupted. We won the relay, and the Water Buffalos won the meet.

The excitement of the meet coming down to the final race fueled the incredible feeling of winning it all. My body was numb as I jumped up and down with my teammates as we celebrated the win. I also remember being embarrassed and shy as people made a big deal about how I swam the final leg of the relay. I didn't want the win to be about me. It was a team victory; I just helped make it happen.

Team wins were more important to me than any individual victory. Whether I was on a winning relay at the age of ten or a part of the Penn State Women's 1983 Eastern Championship Swim Team, I enjoyed contributing to something greater than myself. I never knew the impact that contribution had until my English professor at Penn State showed me the way.

SHOWING UP

Swimming is a winter sport. Spectators at meets usually included family, friends, and classmates. They showed up at Penn State's McCoy Natatorium in their winter coats and quickly stripped them off when they got to the stands. The Nat—as we called it—was super humid, warm, and had that familiar heavy smell of chlorine.

I had a swim meet on a Saturday, and it was one of those typically cold, overcast, and snowy January days in State College, PA. As I was warming up in the pool, I looked up and saw my English professor in the stands with a friend. My class was large, but I got to know my professor because I had to let her know if I were to miss class for an away meet. One day in class, she mentioned she wanted to come to a meet, but I was still surprised to see her there. It was special to me that she was willing to spend part of her weekend to come watch me swim.

In retrospect, that's what humble leaders do. She cared enough about me to support me on a cold Saturday afternoon. Professor Barbara Metzger-Anderson sat through the long meet, which is real dedication for a casual observer.

Although she never told me, I think she came to support me because she knew I had lost my father in December and my coach at home was in intensive care. She cared about me and wanted to show her support outside of the classroom.

A few days later, I received a letter in the mail.

Inside the envelope was the most eloquent note recounting her experience and observations of the meet. She wrote, "Spirit among your swim team members seemed to feel strong to each of you. Your record seemed to impress others more than it did you. Remember how you left the water at that point and used a pocket camera to take candid photos of other swimmers? They wanted to shake your hand, and you were too busy to expect the congratulations. I thought you showed experience as a winner."

"Your coach at home would expect the good sportsmanship you show—grinning words of encouragement to others, full attention to the coach's review of the schedule, and comments she made to you after the record swim."

Her letter had a big impact on me, and it still does, even after all these years. I didn't understand the significance of it at the time, but now I do. Through her unsolicited feedback, I was able to see myself in a way I hadn't been able to before.

When self-doubt creeps in and I question my authenticity as a leader, I remember her letter, and say to myself, "No Katy, it's always been there. It's who you are."

I may not have known it when I was young, but I was humble; it just took my professor showing up at a meet for me to realize it. I also learned that sometimes we don't know the impact we have on others, but I do know that one simple act of kindness had a lasting and profound effect on me.

CHAPTER 19

Promotions
(Langley: 1992)

———

When I was a junior officer, I worked hard, and I played hard. That changed when I got promoted to a general service (GS)-14 mid-level manager.

Back in Asia, when I wasn't scuba diving, I would spend time with my friends eating out, listening to music, shopping, and exploring the city. I often spent time with Sean Healy and a couple of his buddies. They usually visited for a couple of days, and we went out every night they were in town. We would go out for dinner before hitting the bars hard at night. We listened to music, danced, and drank beer, often until 2:00 a.m. I'd be at work by 7:30 a.m. even after a night of staying out way too late.

I became a champion napper. A good thirty-minute nap, and I'd be back at the office ready to go for the rest of the day. I perfected the art of the power nap when I was at Penn State, and it served me well when Sean came to visit.

As a junior officer, I could get my work done and then go have fun with my friends. I didn't realize how good I had it at the time.

I was successful in my first Asian assignment, and that led to new opportunities for positions—and promotions—with increasing responsibility upon my return to Langley. Success as a first-tour officer was measured by meeting the requirements of the position, fulfilling my duties, and practicing sound security practices in both my professional and personal life.

I was shy about my promotions, often keeping the information to myself and not openly celebrating them. That's partially because of my fear of upsetting others who weren't promoted. While I wasn't motivated by the title or the promotion, I appreciated being recognized for a job well done. They were also important because I thrived with new challenges. Each promotion meant I was eligible for positions with increased complexity and responsibility.

When I worked in the HQS area, I attended my promotion ceremonies; I think I missed more of them than I attended because of my time overseas. The ceremonies were always simple with opening remarks from the director of logistics. He gave us his performance expectations at the new level. Then, one by one, we were called up to receive our certificate of promotion that promptly went into a safe because we couldn't take it home.

This was how all my promotions went until I reached GS-14. This promotion was significant and special to me because I was now a mid-level manager. I had goose bumps all over my body when I received the call; I couldn't believe the good news. A rush of excitement came over me as I thought, *I've made it, I've made it... if I never see another promotion, I'll be okay.* A sense of financial security came with this promotion, but it was more than that. At the GS-14 level, I would be managing larger groups and more complex logistics activities. I was a good leader, and I wanted the opportunity to continue to influence others at this level. When I started my career as a GS-7, I never expected to make it to the GS-14 level.

I wore a bright red double-breasted wool dress with gold buttons and a navy and white scarf around my neck to the promotion ceremony. As I sat there, I kept thinking, *I can't believe I'm here.* The director of logistics talked about the importance of mid-level managers and the responsibility for leading others. His talk drove home the message I tried to live by: Good leadership was important to the mission, but it was vital to the people we were leading.

I couldn't help but think how proud Dad would be if he knew I made it to GS-14, the rank he was when he died. There were more promotions to come in my career, but none were as special as the one to GS-14. There was something exciting about knowing I already achieved more than I expected and realizing there was a possibility for more, including up to senior leadership positions.

The GS-14 promotion was significant because it meant I made it beyond the journeyman level in logistics. I would be asked to take on more leadership responsibilities as I was moving into the senior ranks of logistics officers. There was a nice pay increase that came with moving into the GS-14 level, which meant I no longer had to eat canned Progresso soup for dinner. All kidding aside, the promotion gave me a sense of financial security that I welcomed as a single woman.

It is important to celebrate successes in life. Whether those successes are major or minor, it is important to pause and take in the moment, even if it's a quiet celebration with a hike in the mountains or dinner with close friends.

CHAPTER 20

Divorce, a Humbling Experience (Virginia: 2010)

I was a shy kid, and my face often turned red when I was uncomfortable or the center of attention. It was unseasonably warm on my sixteenth birthday. When I arrived home from getting my driver's license, a few of my girlfriends were waiting for me on the porch. Surprise parties weren't the norm in our house, so I didn't expect it. I blushed with embarrassment when I walked up and saw my friends waiting for me.

We hung out on the porch. It was like sitting in a tree house with open windows on all sides, and the leaves were green and beautiful. My friends and I were talking about what we wanted to do when we grew up and boys. As we sat around the table, I made a declaration that I was *never* going to get married. I'm not sure why I said it, but I said it forcibly, and it stuck with me for many years.

Fast forward, and I'm in my late-thirties, stationed in Europe. I met a guy at work, and we became good friends. I admired the way he single-parented his two children and their beautiful dog named Tinto. Spending time with them came naturally as we enjoyed cooking meals together, exploring the city, walking Tinto, going to farmer's markets, and doing fun things together.

Marriage was not something I ever dreamed of, but Glen was my best friend and I said yes when he asked me to marry him. I wanted to spend the rest of my life with him, and I loved his kids. I wanted them to be a part of my life and vice versa.

I knew it wouldn't be easy helping to raise two kids who weren't my own, but I was used to doing anything I put my mind to, and I was confident I could do this. I didn't go into the marriage blindly. In fact, I studied tips on how to be a good stepparent and strategies for blending families. I read every book I could get my hands on, and I thought I was prepared to face any challenges that came my way.

I was two months shy of my fortieth birthday.

On my wedding day, my oldest brother, Michael, walked me down the aisle. I remember telling him how happy I was and that I wasn't afraid of marriage or of raising stepchildren. I was confident in my decision to marry Glen and creating a home for our new family. It felt like the right thing to do.

The first year of marriage was filled with unpacking boxes, merging two households, and settling the children into their new schools. It took six months to find a rhythm that included taking care of the house, juggling schedules, and working in a demanding job in the wake of the September 11 attacks. We had one goal and that was to eat dinner as a family every night.

A couple of years into the marriage, our relationship shifted, and it wasn't what I expected. I was unhappy and felt alone. Even though I was living in a home with a husband, two kids, and our pets, Tinto and Venus, I had never felt so alone in my life. Mealtimes that used to be fun were filled with bickering. Conversations happened around me, and I wasn't a part of them. I was an outsider in my own home, and our connection was gone.

I tried every communication tactic on Earth and some of the strategies I read in those books, and nothing worked long term. I realized it was time to get help; I couldn't do this alone. I found a therapist who came highly recommended. It took me a while to muster the courage to set up an appointment with her, not only because I didn't like to ask for help, but because I was nervous what work might say. The CIA has specific requirements for continued access to classified material; stable mental health was required. I didn't want to do anything to jeopardize my security clearance. In hindsight, my fear was short-sighted because the CIA encourages employees to get help before issues spin out of control. In fact, they have a robust Employee Assistance Program, which I referred other employees to when necessary.

I sat in an overstuffed chair covered in navy-blue plaid fabric in my therapist's office. Her office was cozy and warm. She asked me point blank, "Are you ready to get divorced, or are you trying to make your marriage work?" I let her know I really wanted to make it work, and I didn't plan to give up easily. "All I need is some professional help to navigate the discord." I wanted someone to tell me I wasn't crazy.

I didn't get married to get divorced, and I wanted to be happy in my marriage. I worked with my therapist for almost a year, and there were peaks and valleys in terms of results at home. Even when things were looking up, I continued to feel a low-grade sadness that went from my heart to a pit in my stomach. I lived with a persistent dull ache in my heart.

In between visits to my therapist, I went to church and I prayed. It seemed no matter what I did, life at home went up and down. Things got better for a short time, but then they turned difficult again. Glen and I married in 2001, and it was in 2008 when I finally realized I wasn't meant to be this unhappy. I'd say to myself, "God doesn't want people to be this unhappy." I had to remind myself to not worry about what others thought, and to ignore the teachings of the Catholic Church. I knew I was doing a disservice to Glen and his children by staying.

I was embarrassed my marriage and family life was failing, so I internalized my grief, loneliness, and full-on embarrassment. No one in my family or close circle of friends had gone through a divorce, so I was afraid to talk to them about it. Perhaps I was afraid they would say, "Katy, you signed up for this." In addition to living with the conflict at home, I was in demanding senior executive positions at the CIA, with their own share of conflict. As challenging as my positions were at the CIA, the conflicts at work were easier than those at home.

I was kidding myself thinking people didn't know what was going on. Meanwhile, the voice in my head got louder. "Katy you should have known better than to marry someone with young kids." "Katy, there's something wrong with you." "Katy, you can work through this. You can do it." But I couldn't.

I consulted with my therapist, and we developed a strategy for me to discuss a divorce with Glen. I was sure I wanted a divorce, but I had trouble mustering the courage to tell Glen. She suggested I broach the subject in a public place because our conversations often turned into ugly screaming matches, with comments that caused pain. I didn't feel safe when Glen and I had disagreements, especially when no one else was home.

I vividly remember our lunch as if it was yesterday. I was wearing a white shirt and bright yellow shorts, and I drove us to the restaurant in my car, a silver Saab with a navy-blue convertible top. I took a deep breath when we arrived for sushi. I was extremely nervous, and my heart raced at one hundred miles an hour. I really didn't know if I was courageous enough to have the conversation, but I kept saying to myself, "Have faith, just have faith."

I began to talk. I explained to Glen I thought it would be best if we got divorced. In that moment, I was so grateful to be in a public place because the conversation didn't escalate as it might have had we been at home. The conversation was intense as we sat across from each other in a booth. "Katy, I don't want to get divorced. If it's what you want, then I'll go through with it, but you'll have to file the paperwork."

Before I filed the paperwork, we made a last-ditch effort and went to a marriage boot camp called New Beginnings. They statistically had a 75 percent success rate; three out of four marriages survived long term after the workshop.

The elderly couple who facilitated the weekend pulled us aside on the second day and said, "We rarely say this to couples, but we want you two to make it. There is something special about you two." They gave me hope, but it was short-lived. The boot camp was in October 2008, and we returned home with new tools and lots of homework to do. Communication, communication strategies, and most importantly, a commitment to make mutual decisions.

New Beginnings was over, and within three months, we had fallen back into our old patterns, and nothing changed. That's when I realized I'd done everything I could possibly do to make our marriage work. Yes, we could limp along, but the reality was I was miserable, I no longer trusted my husband, and the love was gone.

It was clear things weren't going to get better. This time, it was easier to tell Glen I wanted a divorce. It wasn't easy, but it was easier than the first time I broached the subject with him.

I often say getting divorced humbled me more than anything else in my life. Until then, I had pretty much been able to do whatever I put my mind to. I made things work.

I couldn't make my marriage work.

I have good friends who helped me through the period of grief both before and after my divorce. Years later they asked me, "Katy, would you do it again?" and I said, "Yes," because without that experience, I wouldn't be who I am today. It humbled me. I also learned that sometimes I can't make things happen no matter how hard I try.

My divorce was the beginning of learning to choose for myself. It was the first time in my life I'd really gone against my religious upbringing—the marriage *and* the divorce—and did something so different from my family. With the help of friends and a therapist, I realized I didn't have to stay in the marriage just because I thought I had to or be married for life.

Sometimes I stick with things too long. My pattern is to do anything I can to make something work, just so I make it work. I've come to know that can be a detriment to myself and others involved. The divorce was the beginning of learning to take a step back or leave when something or someone isn't serving me.

Marriage was hard work, harder than anything I did at the CIA. I could fix a lot of problems in the office but not in my marriage. I said I would do it again, not for the experience of it, but because it was the beginning of finding my voice. I had to use my voice to initiate and go through the divorce.

It also taught me that I didn't have to succeed at everything I did. I was free to make a choice and look out for my well-being, and I learned to be humble when something I thought I could master turned out to be something I couldn't.

PART 7

LOUD TO BE STRONG

CHAPTER 21

You Don't Have to Be Loud to Be Strong (Langley: 2009)

———

I had a misconception about leadership when I began my career at the CIA. I thought I had to be loud and boastful to lead because that was the style of the male leaders I worked with early on in my career. There were far fewer women leaders in the Agency, and most of them were battle-axes. You know, women who were sharp-tongued, combative, tough, and led like one of the guys.

I believe the women leaders I met early in my career thought they had to act like the men to be successful. They not only acted like the men, but they also dressed like them. The women leaders at the Agency, and women in general, tended not to dress with style and a feminine touch but instead wore the "uniform" of navy-blue polyester suits with matching navy-blue military-style pumps. It was the simplest way for women to fit in with their male colleagues—like how the military uses camouflage to cover soldiers to make them blend in with their surroundings.

I thought, *That's not me, and if that's what it takes, I don't want to be in leadership.* I'm not loud; I'm naturally quiet. It takes concerted effort for me to talk loudly, and it tires me out. Instead, I talk softly, and I am a good listener. I'm genuinely curious about others, so I ask questions and listen. Knowing what questions to ask and then deciding what to do is the deepest form of listening.

I found myself being asked to lead whether I was quiet or not and whether I was in a leadership position or not. That's when I realized I didn't really have a choice; I was called to lead. Leadership opportunities came to me organically, and I needed to embrace a style that was authentic to me.

My propensity for quiet was compounded by the fact that I worked in intelligence and couldn't talk about many aspects of my work. So, I became adept at turning a conversation around so it wasn't about me. Whenever I was asked the inevitable question, "What do you do, Katy?" I was quick to respond, "I'm in logistics, and I move boxes around the world." Within a minute the other person's eyes glazed over, and the subject changed.

I used this tactic not just to change the subject about my work, but when people ask questions about me. I tend to be reserved and introverted, as I've never been comfortable talking about myself. In addition to my desire to learn more about others, it preserves my desire to go unnoticed.

Going unnoticed also allows me to do one of my other favorite things: read a room so I understand what is really going on. It was a skill I used as a child and got better at as I went through life. My boss, the director of logistics, once told me I could read a room better than anyone he knew. I was good at it because I practiced it, and at different times in my life, it kept me safe.

There's so much more going on when people are talking beyond what they say. The art of reading a room comes through observing body language, who is meeting with who before or after a meeting, and who is monopolizing the conversation. Where do people sit; are they punctual; do they avoid eye contact, smile, take notes; are they alert, engaged, or do they fall asleep?

I understand the underlying conversations and reactions people are having when I pay attention to nonverbal cues. It's an important skill because it helps me understand people and their motivations. What are people saying when they aren't speaking it aloud? One way it benefits me is that it allows me to evaluate the best way to approach someone and get a read on who they are and how they see the world. It also helps me build trust with others.

I strive to get along with others and see their perspectives; that is until I see someone being treated unfairly, disrespected, or I witness inequitable standards. It always bothered me when I saw kids bullied in school. It also bothered me that I wasn't courageous enough to confront the bullies. I was confident enough to befriend the person being picked on but often unable to address the situation directly with the perpetrator.

The same sinking feeling came over me when I saw people bullied at work. Although a bully at work was a bit more sophisticated, and it wasn't as obvious. It also required skill to manage adult bullies because they've had a lot of practice.

It's imperative for a leader to manage these situations not only for the person directly affected, but for the good of the whole.

A great example of this was when I was the base chief at one of our facilities and the first female in the position. I was responsible for running a large logistics facility, and my civilian counterpart was a former military colonel. I was technically the base chief, but he was the public face of the facility and had been in his position for many years. He took advantage of his long tenure to manipulate and demean others and retain control of the operations.

He had a reputation that preceded him, so I was on the lookout when I arrived. I can't give too many specifics, but he was one of the most talented gaslighters I ever knew. He had a way of manipulating someone by psychological means into questioning their competence and sanity. I observed patiently and watched him treat people poorly for a while, until one day, I'd had enough. It needed to stop.

He had perfected the art of drive-by meetings with me, timing them perfectly for when he knew I only had a few minutes. To avoid that, I scheduled this meeting with him on my terms and arranged it in advance. The discussion was lengthy, and it was just the two of us. I stayed calm, and I followed the agenda I had created.

Essentially, I gave him my expectations for how we would manage people and run the base. I also laid out new reporting requirements for him. I knew he would resist, but going forward, I would hold him accountable for his actions and his treatment of base personnel.

He took copious notes, and he left my office. The next day, he came by for our new daily morning meeting. His face was pale, his eyes were swollen, he looked tired, and his shoulders were slumped. He looked at me and said, "I got home last night and realized I just got the biggest ass-chewing of my career, and you did it in such an unassuming and gentle way." He went on to say that in all his years in the military, and as a civilian, he'd never been dressed down as severely as I had done, and he didn't realize it as it was happening.

He was a big bully.

I understood what was happening because I consistently read the room whenever we were together. I observed his interactions with others, which allowed me to interpret his motivations and the impact he was having on the workforce. The information I gleaned by reading the room helped me prepare for how to approach him and manage the situation.

This experience reinforced for me that you don't have to be loud to be strong, and you don't have to be a bully to be effective. It also taught me a leader must manage these situations not only for the person directly affected but for the good of the whole. I regret I didn't do more for the bullied when I was younger. I did, however, eventually find an effective way to stand up to bullies without becoming like them.

CHAPTER 22

People Underestimate Me (Colorado: 2019)

———

I learned to stand up to bullies for others, but I wasn't good about doing it for myself. I was brought up to put others first and treat people with kindness, but I didn't stand up for myself. I had a lot to learn.

I was raised in a home where religion was an important part of everyday life. I was taught to say my prayers every night, and meals started with a blessing. I had five great-aunts who were nuns, and we visited them regularly at St. Mary's Convent in Pennsylvania. The nuns had been educated as teachers, librarians, and nurses. They would regale my brothers and me with stories of their students, family history and life in a convent on our visits. The fun part of visiting them was playing marathon card games at night.

Many of the beliefs I lived with were passed down from the Catholic Church. Sex before marriage was forbidden, no divorce, don't eat meat on Friday, confess your sins to a priest, you can't eat food before receiving communion, and Sundays were meant for church and donuts.

I never understood why my Aunt Mary, a devout Catholic, had to sit in the back row of church each Sunday and wasn't allowed to take communion. These restrictions were because she married someone who was divorced.

While I'm grateful I was raised with a belief in God, as I got older, my thoughts shifted. I was less interested in organized religion and more interested in my relationship with God. The Catholic Church certainly had a long list of things I couldn't do and a long list of what I needed to do to get into heaven. I kept asking myself, where is the love? Where is the love that is Jesus? Isn't the true meaning of being a follower of Christ to love others as Jesus loved?

Glen was my first and only husband. I'd been going to Catholic Church out of habit since college, and I wanted to get married in a church. While I knew "the rules," we decided to consult with a Catholic priest to see if he would agree to marry us. I thought maybe things were different in 2001, and besides, Glen had been divorced for over ten years at the time. Father explained that the only way we could get married was to annul Glen's previous marriage, which meant time and money, and I couldn't figure out on what grounds his marriage would be annulled. How do you say a marriage never took place when someone has two children? I thought, *No way, we aren't going through the annulment process*, and Glen agreed.

Glen and I were unanimous; going to church was important for our family, so we joined a Methodist Church after our wedding. The lovely old white church was located right on the corner by our house. In many ways, the Methodist Church was like the Catholic Church with the same songs, similar sermons and the same weak coffee served on Sunday mornings. The main difference was the person preaching at the Methodist Church was a minister—who had a wife—dressed in regular clothes and not a priest dressed in a cassock with a white collar—who had no wife.

I started to realize that a church is a building and people were an important part of the church and its community, but I didn't need that to have a relationship with God. I began to understand that my faith and connection to God got stronger the more time I spent in prayer, meditation, and walks with my dog, Grace, in the beautiful mountains of Colorado.

These thoughts led me to join a mindfulness program and learn once more that I don't have to be loud to be strong.

SOFT YET FIERCE

Sometimes, people underestimate me. When my fierce side comes out, it can surprise people because it isn't loud. My "fierce" only comes out when necessary—when the mission demands it or when people are being taken advantage of.

One of those times came shortly after I retired from the CIA. I was curious about what was next in my life, and I was persuaded to join a mindfulness program because of my desire to grow as a person. The program I joined was a personal development program led by a charismatic founder who built a high-demand organization.

I attended programs, and it wasn't long before the founder asked me to develop a book group program for his "non-profit side of the organization." He wanted to leverage my years of experience. He also recognized my genuine care for others and my desire to see people thrive.

The goal of the book group program was to help people transform their lives using the book written by the founder as the guide for learning. I was *all in* because the program tied to my purpose of serving the greater good.

The founder emphasized, "Katy, you will have greater impact and serve others if you lead the effort to grow the book group program, which I intend to move into the non-profit side of my organization."

I was pressured to donate countless hours—more than I care to admit—to build the program and train the trainers. In addition, I mentored members of his leadership team as an additional duty. All of this was required in the capacity of a volunteer.

I developed the robust book group program with the help of other volunteers. It was extremely successful, and it became the primary feeder for the founder's paid programs. As I spent more time near the founder and his inner circle, I was able to see firsthand how he bullied people and mismanaged resources under the guise of philanthropy. I often asked myself if he was hurting people and then it became clear. I was volunteering my time and expertise not to help people but to make the founder visible and wealthy.

When I became aware of what was really happening, I knew it was time to go.

I scheduled a meeting with the founder and told him I was stepping down and it was time for someone else to lead the book program. I was surprised when he easily agreed, and we discussed timing and a transition plan. I should have known what was coming.

A few days later, I attended a mandatory meeting with nearly one hundred apprentices and trainers of the organization. First thing in the morning, the founder announced I was leaving my position as the national director of book groups. When I returned from a working lunch, he initiated a confrontation with me when he called me out in front of the entire group for not being loyal to him.

I was subjected to a verbal reprimand that was harsher than anything I experienced in thirty-two years with the CIA, or in my life. I had previously witnessed him behave this way with others, and now it was with me. I regretted not speaking up during those times. This was my chance.

When it happened to me, I was stunned at first and then I kept reminding myself to breathe. As I breathed and gathered myself, I waited for an opportunity to respond to his verbal assault. As I stood there facing him, I looked straight into his eyes, and with a calm voice, I said, "I don't trust you. I have come to learn you are all about the money; you don't really care about people."

The room was so quiet you could hear a pin drop.

In my four years with the organization, no one had challenged him in this way for fear of inevitable future retaliation. Typically, people just took the harsh criticism and public humiliation. I chose to confront him in a way that showed my leadership. I also hoped my courage and strength would inspire others to see what was truly happening in the organization.

I knew it was time to leave the organization. I was the first person on the leadership team to leave, and I left gracefully. My departure opened the door for others, and it created a tidal wave of departures of apprentices and trainers.

At times, I question how I let myself get involved with such an organization or why I didn't see what was happening sooner. I've come up with lots of reasons, but the one that makes the most sense to me is that I was looking to serve, and I wanted to be part of a team. I thought I had enough power and influence to change the culture. I was forced to realize I didn't.

I was in transition when I encountered the program, and I wanted to belong to an organization that was helping people. I think I did help people but not in the way I initially set out to. I helped some people find the courage to leave the organization, and once they left, I helped some of them process through their feelings of betrayal and grief.

My experience with this program was a turning point. Until then, one of the hardest things for me to do was to stand up for myself. In that moment, I dug deep and found it within me to confront the bully in the Katy McQuaid way. I overcame adversity even when I wasn't in a position of authority, and I was able to assist others through my quiet, direct, and grace-filled approach. Even though I wasn't in a designated leadership position, people trusted me to guide them through their own departures. I was a trusted advisor to help others safely depart the organization.

CHAPTER 23

Dare to be Different (Langley: 2004, 2007)

———

I love clothes and have since I was a kid. One of my favorite pieces was a Calvin Klein jean skirt. I didn't always know how to dress, but I enjoyed getting a couple of new outfits in the fall before school started. My mom was always a sharp dresser, and she still looks stylish at ninety years old.

I'm named after my maternal grandmother, whom I never met, but I wish I had. I learned she loved fashion too. She didn't have many clothes, but what she wore was fashionable. My mom describes her as looking stunning in a powder blue belted wool coat with a blue fur collar that accentuated her blue eyes and tiny waist—along with wearing a hat that made her eyes pop.

My grandmother was also an accomplished painter in her short forty-two years of life. I realize that in addition to my love of fashion, I am gifted with her creative side.

I share about my love of fashion because as I grew more confident, I wore clothes that were colorful. In college, I wore JAMS shorts made of bright floral fabric that matched my first pair of "real" sunglasses. They were the most expensive thing I'd bought myself at that point in life. I'm sure I spent many hours on the lifeguard stand to pay for those red Vaurnets.

That was the true me; I enjoyed wearing fun clothes. All of that had to change when I joined the CIA. There, navy-blue polyester suits were what all the women wore. It allowed us to blend in, be less feminine, and disappear into the background. On occasion, I might have added a pop of color with a pink blouse. That is, until I hired someone to teach me to dress, midway through my career.

I worked with Lauren Rothman, and her goal was to empower women through dress. Recently returned from my tour in Afghanistan, I was heading into a new base chief position.

Lauren asked, "Katy, what do you want people to see when they meet you?"

I said, "My goal is to be understated yet elegant. I want my staff to know I'm in charge, but in a subtle way."

Lauren was the ultimate fashion consultant. Her dress sense was impeccable, yet her approach was relaxed and fun, making it very easy for me to get on board with her ideas.

She started with, "Katy, this is a process; you must wear clothes that fit you. You can't wear clothes that are baggy and too big."

There I was, seated in a dressing room in Nordstrom as Lauren brought me clothes to try on. She suggested a monochrome look with matching pants and shirt topped with a "third piece." My first new outfit was brown well-fitted pants, a brown top, a long green sweater, and shoes with a kitten heel. It was a sharp outfit, and I wore it until it was threadbare.

I dared to break free from tradition to start wearing fashionable clothes. My new look conveyed strength, yet it wasn't loud. It was Humble Yet Fierce and so it matched my inner self.

Working with a style expert taught me to understand and appreciate the power of style.

SOME HABITS ARE HARD TO CHANGE

There were a few habits of mine that were hard to change. One of them was showing up with wet hair. I often went to the gym before work. Just like in my swimming days, I never took the time to dry my hair.

I usually walked into office of logistics conferences at the start of the day with wet hair. The guys got used to me coming in like that, and it was something they teased me about for over twenty years. They'd say, "Here comes McQuaid again with her wet hair." I changed the wet hair habit after working with Lauren, but it was a hard one to break.

The other habit that didn't change was keeping my cars for a long time.

One day, I was driving into the parking lot of an off-site in the mountains when I was the deputy director of logistics. As I pulled into the lot, it was filled with a bunch of fancy new cars. Shiny red pickup trucks, white jeeps, and a few BMWs. I smiled to myself as I parked, thinking *What's wrong with this picture?* My ten-year-old champagne-colored Volvo 850 was in great shape, and it had low miles. It was a sturdy and dependable car. I loved it.

The junior officers stood there looking at me, and if I could read their minds, I think I would have heard, *Our boss drives a stodgy old car like that?*

I haven't changed. I drove a fancy black BMW SUV for a short time but sold it within a few months; it just wasn't me. I decided to stay with my reliable and trustworthy 2006 Acura MDX that was perfect for my road trips with Grace.

As leaders, sometimes it's easier to go with the flow than stay true to yourself. I did it at times in my career until I realized it wasn't sustainable. When I wasn't true to myself, life got harder and more uncomfortable. That's why it's so important to stay true to yourself and dare to be you. Your overall well-being and happiness depend on it, and others will strive to follow your example.

PART 8

FIND YOUR VOICE

CHAPTER 24

Finding Your Voice (New York and Virginia: 1970s)

Sometimes, the words just wouldn't come out of my mouth. That's when I learned the power of pen and paper.

"Those boots are for boys, and you are not allowed to wear them to school." That's what the principal, wearing a black cloth habit, said as I walked into St. Stephen's School in the fourth grade. She scolded me for wearing desert boots. They were popular in the '70s—light tan suede boots with laces that went up to the ankle.

I wore my boots with a uniform of a white blouse with a green and gold plaid skirt and knee socks. They were new, and I absolutely loved them. I didn't get new clothes very often, and when Sister told me I wasn't allowed to wear them to school anymore, I was crushed.

How was I going to tell my parents I wasn't allowed to wear my new boots to school? Well, I didn't tell them, and when I went to school the next day, I planned to hide my shoes behind a piece of posterboard as I walked from the bus to my classroom. My plan failed. Sister was waiting for me at the front door, and this time, she had a ruler in her hand as she yelled at me. "I told you you're not allowed to wear those shoes into this school." The ruler found its way to the back of my legs and ankles. This time, Sister called my parents and told them my shoes were inappropriate for a young lady to wear to school.

My parents transferred me from St. Stephens Catholic School to Huth Road Elementary School in fifth grade. The experience with the ruler was traumatic for me, and I didn't know how to tell my parents what happened. I realize now how often I kept quiet when I needed to speak up. What could have happened if Sister hadn't called my parents? Would the beatings have gotten worse? Would I have started to act out or feign illness? I don't know, but I'm grateful I didn't have to find out.

As a young child, I didn't know how to speak up. It was something I had to learn, one step at a time, and it began with a letter.

AN IMPORTANT LETTER

I started swimming in 1968 when my family lived in San Antonio, Texas, because my dad was stationed there for a year. It was a way for my parents to keep all five kids involved in one activity. I was the youngest member on the swim team.

When we moved back to Grand Island, New York, my parents would drive us about thirty minutes to practice in Buffalo. It was a big deal when I got my first team swimsuit at nine years old with the Water Buffalo swim team. My suit was navy-blue with gold panels down the side and a patch with the team logo in the shape of a crest sewn on the front.

I was a dedicated swimmer, and I loved it so much. I spent hours at practice perfecting each stroke as I cut through the water. Every stroke provided an opportunity for me to fine tune the way I moved my arms through the water and kicked my legs. I focused on the black line at the bottom of the pool, and I enjoyed the quiet time that came along with each mile I swam. My dad was transferred from New York to McLean, Virginia.

My parents didn't have a lot of money at the time, so they signed me up to swim with the Military District of Washington (MDW) swim team because it was free. It didn't take me long to figure out that the coach, Colonel Kelly, was tough. Practices were held in Arlington Hall, a historic facility that was once a school. The grounds were beautiful; the buildings were dated. The four-lane pool was dingy, and the air was warm and humid. The locker rooms were made with concrete floors, and it felt like I was walking on rough sandpaper.

When Col Kelly coached the team, she yelled and belittled me and my teammates. She even used a seatbelt with the metal clasp to hit us if we weren't doing something right in practice. I would watch the belt in her hands with each stroke as I turned my head to breath. When I saw it coming, I ducked under the water so she wouldn't hit my head. Sometimes the buckle landed on my body and would leave a red mark.

Col Kelly taught me early on what *not* to do when coaching or leading others. I'm simply not motivated by that type of teacher or coach. Instead, I respond well to constructive feedback and coaching. Sometimes, it's not the words or what's being said; it is the energy behind it. I could feel the judgement and anger coming at me when Col Kelly tried to berate or shame me into correcting my stroke or swimming faster.

I had to get off the team. As much as I loved swimming, the practices were unbearable because of the abuse. I didn't know how to talk to my parents about it, so I decided to write them a letter.

I sat at the desk that looked out my bedroom window onto green grass and large oak trees in our front yard. I took out a lined yellow pad of paper and pen, wondering if I had the courage to give my parents a letter. I decided this was so important I had to write the letter asking them to please let me swim for the private Solotar Swim Team. It meant they would have to start paying dues.

In the letter, I focused on my desire to work with a coach and teammates who were world class. I told my parents I didn't ask for much, but it was important for me to be able to train with Coach Solotar. I didn't have the courage to tell my parents about the abuse from Col Kelly. I just focused on the fact that I would become a better swimmer with Solotar.

I poured my heart into the letter but was afraid to give it to my parents. I tiptoed out of my room that night after everyone went to bed and left the letter on the kitchen table for my parents to find the next morning. My parents discussed the letter with me and made the decision to let me join the Solotar Swim Team. It turned out to be an incredible move for me because I swam for Coach Solotar, Jean Rachner, and Tom Healy. They were all top-notch coaches—Mr. Solotar coached the US swimming team in the Maccabean and Pan Am Games, along with other international meets. We had inspiring Olympians on our team, including Melissa Belote with three gold medals and Margie Moffet with a World Record.

Mr. Solotar and his coaches believed in doing your best and working hard. They taught me that each race was against myself; it wasn't about beating another person. My victories were their victories, and my losses were their losses. They created a safe environment where I could grow and thrive not only in the pool but in life.

The environment at Solotar was much better for me. There were hours and hours of practice—one practice before school and another in the afternoon—and my alarm clock went off well before dawn most days. Coach Solotar was very strict about arriving for practice on time. One minute late, and I wasn't allowed in the pool. If I was late and missed a practice, it was excruciating for me, so it didn't happen often. I wanted to be the best I could be, and I hated to miss a practice. No one wants to get up at 4:00 a.m. just to be turned away at the door.

The letter I wrote to my parents was a defining moment in my life. It was the start of finding my voice. I imagine my life would be very different had I not "spoken up" and written that letter. I didn't go into detail about the physical abuse in it, but I conveyed my deep desire to change teams. I never did tell my parents about Col Kelly.

The letter was an effective way for me to communicate my concerns with my parents.

What if I hadn't written the letter? What if I had stayed at MDW? Would I have reached the level of athleticism I did swimming with Solotar? Thankfully, I'll never know the answers to those questions because I found the courage to write that letter.

Finding my voice took a journey of many years. I was a kid who didn't speak up out of fear; I stuffed it all in hoping no one would notice. Then I began to crawl by writing a letter to my parents. The journey was a series of baby steps that led to writing the *Everybody Loves Grace* children's series, *Humble Yet Fierce*, and keynote speaking (McQuaid 2018).

There are many effective ways to find your voice. It can look different for everyone. Just find it any way you can.

CHAPTER 25

Stand in Your Truth (Langley: 2004)

———

I became the deputy director of logistics in 2003 when logistical support to the major conflict zones was really gearing up. We depended on a critical overseas support platform run by a very charismatic and influential leader named Dusty. He was relentless in pursuing a very large contract to a specific company for the movement of *all* air cargo. This contract activity was worth *millions* of dollars.

Pressure came in the form of repeated phone calls over a secure line and an occasional visit from his overseas location to meet with my boss and me. The Agency used multiple vendors to fulfill its growing demand for commercial air shipments. But Dusty kept asking us to sole source the Agency's commercial air shipments to *his* preferred vendor.

With each phone call and visit came a veiled threat that if we didn't do it his way, we would suffer the consequences. My boss and I felt the pressure, and we owed Dusty an answer.

We met with the managers of the Agency's logistics warehouse responsible for the movement of all cargo via commercial air, military air, rail, sea, and truck.

The warehouse team assured us there was no need to sole source the commercial air shipments. While showing us the data, they explained we needed multiple carriers to meet the mission, and the competition between companies made it more cost effective. Bill and I made the decision to continue using multiple providers for the movement of air cargo.

At the same time, we heard rumors that Dusty was going to be promoted to executive director (EXDIR), the number three position in the Agency. We knew our decision wouldn't go over well with Dusty, and we would be taking a significant professional risk by saying no. We also knew our integrity was at stake, but we personally couldn't do it any other way.

Bill and I stayed in alignment with our decision to use multiple vendors. It was the right thing to do for the organization and taxpayers, and it modeled integrity for the workforce. It was the right decision for many reasons—the organization had better commercial shipping options without the sole source, and multiple companies had an opportunity to fairly compete for the business.

In October 2004, shortly after we told Dusty no, he moved into the Agency's EXDIR position. I thought, *This is it, my career is over.* Again and again, I would say, "I have to wake up and be able to look at myself in the mirror every morning." It was also about the workforce; we needed to model integrity to them. They were involved in the due diligence process with us, and our decision meant we were willing to speak truth to power.

I sometimes wonder what would have happened if my boss was someone other than Bill, someone who caved to the pressure. I'll never know for sure what I would have done, but I'm confident I would have escalated my concerns through the appropriate CIA channels.

SOMETIMES YOU JUST HAVE TO WAIT IT OUT

In early 2004, I was selected into a new program for the Agency's top 25 leaders. The program was started by the CIA director who wanted to prepare the Agency's next set of officers for top leadership positions. I was totally shocked when I received notification I was selected into the program. I never thought of myself in that echelon at the Agency. I knew I worked hard and tackled tough issues, but wasn't that standard? I lacked the confidence to see myself in the top 25.

When Dusty became EXDIR, he called together the group of twenty-five. I went into the meeting with trepidation because it was the first time I'd met with Dusty since we made the decision not to sole source to his favored company. I also knew how Dusty liked to make an example of those he didn't like in front of others.

We gathered in a small conference room, and the space was tight, the temperature hot, and the tension thick. I purposely sat in a chair that was lined up against the wall, leaving the chairs at the table open for others. Dusty's reputation preceded him, and many of us who weren't in his inner circle expected the worst. We knew he would dress down someone.

His first victim was me.

Dusty asked the question "What are the Agency's biggest challenges today?" and I decided to answer it. He immediately admonished me in front of the group. I looked him in the eye, but I didn't say a word. Nor did anyone else. The others sat in silence, staring at the table in front of them. Retribution for the decision we made regarding the commercial air contract began.

Shortly after this meeting, Dusty disbanded the group. Probably because he hadn't selected the group of twenty-five—they weren't his people. It worked out in my favor that he disbanded the group because it limited my contact with him. When a logistical issue arose, my boss interfaced with Dusty to protect me. Who knows what the trajectory of my career might have been if the group had stayed intact? But under the new leadership, it was better to reduce my visibility.

Dusty was a big field guy; by that I mean someone who lived for the field. He loved living abroad and being involved in field operations. Dusty had a change of heart about me when I volunteered to go to Afghanistan.

I was a few days away from my departure for Afghanistan when I walked down the hallway near the cafeteria and saw Dusty getting off the elevator. He locked eyes with me and said, "I want to see you in my office before you leave." I didn't have a choice, so I set up a meeting with his admin assistant.

When I got to his office on the seventh floor, it was decorated with dark-cherry wood furniture and many certificates, plaques, family photos, and awards on the walls. As I entered, I noticed his tone was gentler. He offered to make me a cup of coffee, and as he sat down, he said, "I guess I was wrong about you. You know, Katy, several people I really respect in this Agency think the world of you, and I disagreed with them. But now I understand they were right about you, and I was wrong."

I couldn't believe my ears.

That was the last time I saw Dusty. While I was in Afghanistan, Dusty was removed from the HQS building while the FBI searched his office, and helicopters flew over Langley and his home not far down the road. Dusty was eventually convicted of honest services fraud, conspiracy, and money laundering and sentenced to thirty-seven months in federal prison.

Dusty's fall reinforced my decision to say no to his vendor.

This experience taught me how important it is to stand in my truth. There was no promotion or position that was more important to me than my integrity and doing the right thing. I leaned heavily on my faith, and it helped me get through it and empowered me to move forward with confidence.

CHAPTER 26

Staying Strong in Crisis (Denver: 2013)

———

My experience leading a church through crisis was like Capt. Sullenberger's emergency landing of US Airways flight 1549 in the Hudson River on January 15, 2009.

Sullenberger's airplane flew into a flock of Canada geese, and both engines were severely damaged, causing an almost complete loss of thrust. Repeated attempts to restart the engines were unsuccessful. The Pathways Church experience was very similar.

Pathways Church was in the heart of Denver in the historic Temple Events Center located one block from the famous Colfax Avenue. It was a gritty inner city, nondenominational church, filled with young people who flocked to it each week to listen to an inspiring message from its charismatic pastor. Gil Jones talked about everyday life with expertly crafted messages.

The church's mission was to care for the underserved and homeless population in the city. Warm meals were served in the basement on Tuesdays to everyone who came. The pastor claimed Pathways was the "fastest growing inner-city church in America." Whether or not that was true, I'll never know, but he said it all the time.

I started attending Pathways Church after I moved to Denver. My realtor recommended it after I inquired about churches in the area. "Katy, I think you'll enjoy the music and the message. There is a high energy brought by the mostly millennial crowd who attends." The pastor was a gifted communicator, and his weekly messages were filled with humor. They touched a range of emotions—each week felt like he'd written the sermon just for me. I know others felt the same way.

I attended services regularly and slowly got involved in various ministries to make friends outside of work and to help the church. Most of my friends in Denver were people I met through Pathways. The church seemed to grow as each Sunday the room was filled, and new services were added to accommodate the new people.

But some things didn't add up. I watched the staff working and could see they were stressed, overworked, and unhappy. Young women hung on Gil's every word as he preached, and I thought, *This isn't good.* I also sensed the pastor was playing his audience by turning on crocodile tears during his sermons. I knew in my gut that something was wrong; his actions spoke louder than his words. He talked about being a devoted single parent to his four kids in his sermons. Yet he was partying with young congregants after Sunday evening service.

I decided I would keep going to Pathways because this was where most of my friends were. I expressed my concerns to a few close friends, and they agreed with me, but we didn't make any effort to find a new church.

One of my friends, a Pathways church elder, shared his suspicions through trusted conversations with other elders. They were wary of the pastor's conduct with staff and congregants at the church. Based on what they found, they had grounds to fire him. It wasn't a decision they took lightly, but they needed and wanted to protect the staff and other women in the congregation who were most affected by his conduct.

I lived through the experience because I was a sounding board and trusted advisor for my friend throughout the investigation and decision process. Through him, I learned about the elders' marathon meetings and their desire for Gil Jones to get the help he needed. The elders also recognized that members of the congregation—mostly women—and staff were traumatized, and they too needed help. It took courage and strength for the women to speak to the elders about their experiences. There were other women who were too afraid to speak out for fear of experiencing the wrath of Gil's large and loyal following.

Some members of the elder team resigned after Gil was removed. They were tired, and they didn't have the strength to see the church through the transition. A call was placed for nominations for new elders. In the process, someone nominated me, and my initial reaction was "Hell no." I was too busy with my demanding CIA job. I also didn't think I was an appropriate candidate to be an elder because I was divorced. I informed the executive pastor that I was not interested.

A few days later, I was on a morning walk with Grace, and a voice popped in my head that said, *Katy, say yes. You must serve on the Pathways' elder team.* I replied, *No, God, not me. I'm not the right person.* It was as if I was being smacked on the head by a two-by-four. I heard again, *No, you have to serve on the elder team.*

I've learned through the years to listen to these loud and clear messages. I find if I don't listen, the messages just get louder and more direct. I called the executive pastor and let him know I changed my mind and would be willing to serve.

The fun began. Four of us joined the elder team, and I don't think any of us were prepared for what was coming. As we combed through the financial records, we found out the church was in serious debt—all over the city. Pathways hadn't paid the staff, parking lot owners, the mortgage company, associated fines and late fees, the list went on.

The church was in crisis. There is an old commercial for the investment bank, EF Hutton. The commercial says "When EF Hutton talks, people listen." People would say that about me at times, and it happened this was one of those times. My experience at the CIA as a leader of logistics and support operations made me perfectly suited to help guide the team through the church's transition. First thing, I insisted that we must hire a consultant with experience in church transitions. (Yes, unfortunately, it happens more than you would expect.) Thankfully, the other elders agreed, and we hired StepUp Resources to consult with us for a nominal fee.

Our goal was to find a way for the church to continue. Surely, all we needed was to find a new lead pastor who could help us heal and rebuild. As time went on, it became abundantly clear that God's plan was for the church to close. As we dug into the financial records, we uncovered more and more things that were wrong.

The tension, fear, and worry we felt were palpable. We wanted to keep the church afloat financially, and we empathized with the young congregation who wanted to believe in their pastor. Elders are primarily responsible for the spiritual health of a church; the additional duties of meeting financial obligations and operating the church were an added duty for this situation. The congregation was divided into two camps, those that believed in the pastor and were angry he was let go, and those who knew the decision to remove him was for cause (Pendergast 2013).

The elders walked a fine line. We needed to respect the privacy of the women who stepped forward, and yet people wanted to know why the pastor was removed. The inappropriate behavior was not just with women; there were men who were abused and bullied as well. The pastor's inner circle and staff built a level of tolerance for the abuse. There were a few who left but others who were numb to the impact. I've since learned this happens in cults and other unhealthy organizations. Unfortunately, the pastor was extremely charismatic and used it to prey on the innocent.

Josh Hart, a professor of psychology at Union College says, "As to the leaders themselves, they typically present themselves as infallible, confident, and grandiose." Their charisma draws people in, Hart says. And followers who are craving peace, belonging, and security might gain a sense of those things, as well as confidence, through participation in the group (Shane 2022).

Janja Lalich, an expert in cultic studies and Professor Emerita of Sociology at California State University, Chico, notes that in a cult setting, the cognitive dissonance often "keeps you trapped as each compromise makes it more painful to admit you've been deceived." Lalich explains in her TED-ED video: "It uses both formal and informal systems of influence and control to keep members obedient with little tolerance for internal disagreement or external scrutiny" (Shane 2022).

Pathways Church was so far in debt the utility bills weren't paid. As we held meetings in the church office, it was so cold we could see our breath. That's when the elders decided to start holding our weekly meetings in my condo. Our meetings were grueling, both physically and emotionally. We often met after a full day of work until 11:00 p.m. We prayed for guidance as we created the plan for the church transition.

We came to the decision that we must sell the church building, the historic Temple Events Center, just a few blocks from the Colorado State Capital, to pay the debts we owed around Denver. I made a cold call to a real estate attorney and explained the situation. I asked if there was any way her firm would be willing to help us sell the building. They agreed and only charged a small fee.

As the process unfolded, it seemed like every step forward was met with two steps backward. We had to overcome several administrative and legal hurdles just to put the building up for sale. We eventually reached a majority decision among the church members to sell the building. But the elders held a much deeper concern because we knew we had a responsibility to shepherd the congregation through their grief, betrayal, and loss, all while keeping the congregants on their spiritual journey.

The elders racked and stacked the debts owed by Pathways. Truly, it was a story of redemption. We returned down payments to brides who paid a deposit to rent the church for their wedding. We returned $40,000 to a local church whose intended donation was siphoned off for other uses. We paid the parking lot owner, the mortgage company, and the bank fines that had accrued. The staff was given severance pay and reimbursed for counseling expenses.

Each member of the elder board brought their strengths and gifts to the team. Mine happened to be the gift of administrative experience. Even though I was new, it was a great opportunity for me to use my voice. We were in a crisis, and I was confident my experience in the CIA was going to help us navigate through these turbulent times.

On a cold and windy October night, the final church service was held in the sanctuary. The church was filled, every seat was occupied, and there was a hum in the room. Four generations of elders and worship bands paid tribute to Pathways. The elders told wonderful stories of connection, caring, and spiritual growth that took place over the years.

I couldn't have imagined such a lovely night was possible amid the chaos. Months of grueling discoveries, meetings, and challenges ended beautifully. It's not something I want to go through again, but the rewards were great. Through this experience, I learned to trust what I'm seeing, feeling, and knowing. It was another opportunity to use my voice and lead in a humble yet fierce way.

CHAPTER 27

Voice Lessons from Grace (Denver: 2022)

Grace was my beloved Finnish Lapphund (dog) who came to live with me when she was four years old. By that time, she was already a mother to two very large litters of puppies. She was raised on a farm in Canada until the owner's husband complained there were too many dogs on their farm, and one of the dogs "had to leave."

When she first came to live with me in 2011, she didn't know where she fit in. Her new big brother, Tinto, also a Finnish Lapphund, was fifteen years old. When Grace walked into the house for the first time, it was as if she and Tinto had always been together, but there was already a routine, and Grace wasn't sure what her role was. When I picked up their leashes to go on our walks, Grace waited behind Tinto as if to say "you go first." And she always let Tinto eat from the first bowl of food I placed on the floor at mealtime.

Grace instinctively knew Tinto was her elder and that you don't mess with a senior dog's seniority and routine. She let Tinto lead on our slow walks as he showed her all his favorite spots in the neighborhood. She also listened when he taught her the most important rule—you aren't allowed on Mommy's bed.

Grace and Tinto were together for exactly a year. She really loved being with Tinto, and in his final days, Grace would bring his favorite toy to him. She would lay his stuffed Dalmatian next to him before she laid down near him on the floor, or watch over him from my bed when I was at work.

The time with the two of them together was precious. I loved seeing them together. But I also could see Grace was willing to serve her brother and take second place. She quietly watched and observed, and I sensed she wanted to lead. It was only natural because she was the stronger of the two, yet she was careful not to step on Tinto's toes. For example, she didn't try to steal his food or treats. She was so patient with him as he slowed down; she would never push or try to get ahead on our walks.

Grace was always very quiet. Friends and houseguests commented how stealthy she was—quiet when she moved from room to room, and she *never* barked. The rare exception was when she saw a bear on our driveway when we stayed in the mountains.

After Tinto died, Grace realized she could start to ask for things. She did it in subtle ways, like deciding new routes for our walks. Instead of going on our normal slow walk around the block, she started pulling gently on her leash toward a nearby hospital or down Broadway, a very busy Denver street. She also went much farther on our walks.

Grace was stepping into her own, but she still didn't bark.

Grace had a way of looking people in their eyes and letting them know they were loved. And in return, people fell in love with Grace. No matter where we went, people asked to pet Grace, and invariably, as they walked away, they would say, "She just made my day."

I could share story after story about Grace's ability to make people feel loved. From our long walks in the neighborhood to sitting next to a person who was emotionally hurting during a get-together in our condo, Grace had an uncanny ability to know who needed her love, and she sought them out. I called it her magic.

But don't let that fool you. While Grace had an extremely gentle spirit about her, she knew how to be fierce when needed. When another dog was aggressive toward her, my heart jumped into my throat, and I screamed as loud as I could. Grace, on the other hand, was quick to respond to an attack by baring her teeth and fighting back as the dust flew. She knew how to defend herself.

Grace battled ear infections for many years, and as a result, she eventually lost her hearing. I started to notice this when I walked into a room and she didn't know I was there until she could see me. At times, it would startle her, but she got used to it.

Grace was shy at first, but she eventually found her voice in her later years. I noticed Grace started barking as soon as we stepped out of our condo door. She discovered she would get a reaction from our neighbor when she began her new morning routine. I tried to quiet her down, but Grace just looked at me with a big smile on her face. It was almost like she was saying to me, "It's another great day!" I heard myself whispering, "Hey, here comes Dana... let's see if she will play with us today." Grace immediately started running down the hallway and barking loudly into Dana's open arms. Clearly, Grace had found her voice and was not afraid to use it!

Animals are amazing teachers when we pay attention and listen carefully to them. I believe Grace wanted me to use my voice, and she started by encouraging me to tell her story. Grace, the rare barker, started "talking" about the same time I gave my first keynote speech on humble leadership. It isn't a coincidence that she started speaking up at the same time I did.

PART 9

AN ENDING AND
NEW BEGINNINGS

CHAPTER 28

Teamwork
(Denver: 2017)

———

One crisp October morning, as Grace and I were on our walk, she tugged on her leash slightly and pulled me in the direction of Denver Health. When Grace did this, it was a sign that she wanted to do her "rounds" at the hospital.

The captain of the paramedics was walking toward the hospital when he spotted Grace out of the corner of his eyes, and he stopped in his tracks, saying, "This is the prettiest dog I've ever seen." When he leaned down to pet her, Grace looked straight into his eyes and into his heart. Captain Brian uttered, "If only I could start my day like this every day."

Captain Brian's reaction was similar to others we often encountered on our walks. That time, though, it was different. A friend of mine, Beth Nicoson, had been telling me I needed to write a book for years. She would whisper in my ear, "You're supposed to write a book." I ignored Beth's gentle nudges because I didn't think anyone would be interested in my life story. This time, as we left the hospital grounds, I heard a whisper tell me the book I was supposed to write wasn't about me. I was supposed to tell Grace's story.

I thought, *This is crazy.* The whole way home, I argued with God. Then I got inside my condo and the voice wouldn't stop. *That story you're supposed to write is about Grace.* I assumed the book would be a children's book, and I was like, *Really God? I can't do that. I don't even have children.*

As the voice persisted, I thought, *What's the worst thing that can happen?* I could spend twenty minutes a day journaling about Grace and see where it goes. I didn't have to think about it as I blurted out, "I have the title. It's *Everybody Loves Grace.*"

STEP OUT IN FAITH—THAT'S HOW THE GRACE STORIES BEGAN

I committed to write twenty minutes each day, and I had so much fun that twenty minutes of writing often turned into an hour or more. The first manuscript was completed within two weeks. That's when I met with a friend, Katie Mount, and told her about writing Grace's story and that it was meant to be a children's book.

Katie listened carefully and asked, "Have you considered writing the story from Grace's perspective?" Her suggestion was brilliant.

I replied, "I love your idea. I'm going to tell the story through Grace's eyes."

The rewrite didn't take long because I enjoyed it. Even though it was something new, I had *so* much fun imagining how Grace would share her adventures. Journaling was an extension of my daily walks with Grace. I talked to her on our walks, and she gave me certain looks that told me she was up to something. In that, I saw her great sense of humor, so I incorporated her keen wit into the story.

FIND THE RIGHT PEOPLE TO HELP MAKE IT HAPPEN

I started to pray on another morning walk with Grace. *God, if I'm really supposed to publish this book, I need an editor, an illustrator, a publisher, and a printer to help me.*

That's when I decided to give Beth a call and told her I'd written a book, but it wasn't what she thought. I explained to her I'd written a book about Grace. "I don't know how I am going to get it done, but I just prayed, and if it's meant to be, I'll get the help I need."

Beth promptly replied, "I just met someone at an Austin area Chamber of Commerce meeting who is a publishing consultant, and he seems very knowledgeable, maybe he can help you. I'll connect you with him."

The connection to Mel Cohen was invaluable and a key to my publishing the book. Mel read the manuscript and said, "Katy, you have a story." He farmed it out to a couple of editors with extensive publishing experience, and they also said I had a story.

They were impressed with the life lessons I conveyed through Grace's story and wanted me to expand the content. Mel and the other editors suggested more than one Grace story needed to be told; they could see a series. I was a bit overwhelmed by the suggestion since I hadn't published the first book yet. But I knew they were right. There were so many adventures to share, so I decided to go with the flow and see where the first book led.

FIND AN ILLUSTRATOR

Little did I know writing the manuscript would be the easiest part of the process. Once I had the green light that I had a story, I embarked on the next vital part of the process, and that was finding an illustrator.

This was new territory for me and so different than building teams at the CIA. I was out of my element.

I had a vision for what I wanted the illustrations to look like, but I hadn't a clue how to find someone who could turn them into reality. I wanted the illustrations to look and feel like watercolor paintings. It was critical the artist capture Grace's spirit.

My publishing consultant helped me understand the illustrator selection process, which took nearly eight months. I finally found someone who captured the essence of Grace beautifully in her illustrations. This was when I began working with Susan Lavalley.

Susan's done an amazing job with the book illustrations, and they have gotten easier and better as we've progressed through the series. We've gotten to know each other well and developed a synergy that comes with working closely together over time.

A fun part of each book is creating the cover. I learned from others in the book industry that the cover design is a vitally important part of any book. Susan came up with a few ideas for the cover after reading the final manuscript. While I had my own ideas, I preferred to hear Susan's first. She explained her vision, and we discussed it until we came to an agreement on the cover design. It was a collaborative process.

The illustration process with Susan worked seamlessly for all six books. When I think about it, that's how it worked in the CIA when it was time to create something new. My best decisions came when I asked questions and stayed open to new ideas, such as the design and build for the logistics and support hub in Afghanistan. My team presented me with options and new ideas, one that was drawn on the back of a napkin. I went with the flow, and we implemented their idea, and it worked so well the facility endured for fifteen years.

LEAN ON OTHERS WITH EXPERIENCE

It was a big shift going from senior executive to writing a book. Time was of the essence because I wanted Grace to be alive when the books were published. With zero knowledge, I headed down the path of self-publishing. I knew I couldn't do it alone, so I brought in people who could help me. It took a team to get the first *Everybody Loves Grace* book across the finish line, and we've stayed together through the series.

When I started writing the first *Grace* book, I thought maybe there would be three books in the series. The stories came easily as Grace and I went on our road trip adventures. We traveled for the pure enjoyment of it, and a theme would arise from each trip that brought poignant life lessons from Grace.

What's been truly amazing for me as the author is the impact the *Everybody Loves Grace* books have had on children and adults alike. The *Grace* books are helping children learn to read and comforting children with high anxiety. Children from all over the world fell in love with Grace through her books.

My greatest joy comes when I receive feedback from parents of children that have overcome reading difficulties through reading the *Grace* series. Parents tell me about their child who never asked to read before bed, and now they do; or the child who insists the *Grace* books must go with them when they visit their grandparents; or the eleven-year-old child with delayed reading abilities whose mother credits Grace's books with getting her over the hump. The stories are interesting, yet easy enough for each child to read.

The books have a great impact on seniors too. I never saw this coming when I wrote them. A reader in York, Pennsylvania, shared from her assisted living facility, "Katy, you say the books are for kids six to ten years old, but I think you should say they are for people six to ninety-one plus years old. I absolutely love your books. Please keep writing more."

Another family friend, Rita, is in her nineties, and she called to tell me how much she loves the *Grace* books. "Katy, I'm a voracious reader, but there is something special about your stories. I read them repeatedly."

HELPING OTHERS FIND THEIR VOICE HELPED ME FIND MY VOICE

I often get asked to talk to someone who is interested in writing a children's book. I'm more comfortable helping someone else find their voice than I've been in finding my own. The learning process of writing a book has been so rewarding. I encourage others to write if they are even thinking about it.

I met Justine Fedak after a mutual friend of ours asked if I'd speak with her. While talking with Justine about her idea for her *Magic Chair* children's book, we discussed my transition from CIA to children's book author. She insisted I *must* write a book about my experiences as a woman leader in the CIA.

In fact, Justine is the one who came up with *Humble Yet Fierce* as the title for this book. In helping Justine find her voice, it helped me find mine. She made a concerted effort and encouraged me to write a book and share the experiences that shaped my life and leadership style.

WILLINGNESS TO LEARN AND TRY SOMETHING NEW

The *Everybody Loves Grace* books could not have happened without the help of experienced people who were willing to mentor me through the process. It also took help from friends who supported and encouraged me throughout. The impact of the series continues to grow with the books serving as the foundation for the *Living with Grace—A Seniors Program*, designed to provide seniors with a way to engage, connect, and thrive.

It turns out that writing about Grace was easy for me to do. Her books were the first step to getting me comfortable talking about myself. They were the conduit to get me to this book. They opened the door to finding my voice and being able to write about myself.

While the *Grace* books were a shift from the career I knew for thirty-two years, I was willing to take the risk and try something completely new. I am so happy I did. The books opened my heart to people of all ages, and they helped me see the world from a different perspective. Quite simply, writing the *Grace* books changed my life in ways I could never have imagined when I retired. My life continues to be significantly enriched through spreading Grace's lessons of love and kindness with children and seniors.

CHAPTER 29

When Enough is Enough (Pennsylvania Road Trip and Langley: 2015)

With all the traveling I did with the Agency, I rarely spent Thanksgiving in the same place twice. So, when an opportunity came up for a road trip to Pennsylvania with Grace, we both jumped at the chance. This road trip adventure became the fifth book in the *Everybody Loves Grace* series.

The trip took us through seven states from Denver, Colorado, to Bernville, Pennsylvania. I must say, Grace is *the best* travel companion on road trips. I like to call her my copilot because she stays awake the whole time as she watches me from the back seat. I am convinced she doesn't sleep while I'm driving because she wants to be sure I stay awake.

We were excited for the trip, but I wasn't sure how long it would take us because the weather can be dicey in November. I mentioned to Grace we would need to be flexible on this road trip even though we were both anxious to get to Koziar's Christmas Village.

The delays began before we could get out of Denver when a storm dropped nearly a foot of snow the night before our scheduled departure. That was our first flexible moment as we waited until noon to begin the adventure, but the snow made for a beautiful drive. All I could see for miles was pristine white snow covering the flatlands of Kansas. The sky turned pink as the sun started to set, and that made me happy because I was reminded of the old saying: "Pink sky at night, sailor's delight." We were in for a nice day of driving the next day.

Every good road trip requires close coordination with the weather channel. It was the first thing I tuned into when we arrived at our hotel in Salina, Kansas. There was another storm coming behind us from the west, so Grace and I went to bed and planned for an early start the next morning. We had to keep driving to stay in front of the storm.

Our luck held until we were on the outskirts of Pittsburgh. The sky was dark with a freezing rain that covered the curvy and narrow roads. As I drove, 18-wheelers passed by with a blinding spray and wind that pushed our car. I held on tightly to the steering wheel. Grace remained calm in the back seat, all the while keeping her focus intently on me as if to say, "It will be okay; we will get through this." Her calmness helped me stay focused and confident that everything would be okay.

Another storm was predicted by the weather channel, so we hustled in the morning to get started. It turned out we only drove one hour on the Pennsylvania Turnpike before I had to pull off the road because it was sleeting and the road was covered in ice. We were only two hours from Koziar's, but I had to check us into another hotel because the ice storm was going to last all day.

We arrived at Koziar's the next day in time for the book signing, even though the weather delayed our arrival by two days. As anxious as I was to get to our destination, I knew when to pull over and stop for the night. Grace and I met some wonderful families, teachers, and children, and the book signing was a big success. The trip cross-country was an important lesson to be flexible and a reminder I needed to do more of it in everyday life.

This road trip was analogous to my career with the Agency. I would be headed in one direction and then circumstances would lead me to adjust along the way. Through most of my career, I was able to find my way through or around the storm and find purpose and adventure in the more challenging moments.

There is a level of stress associated with working in intelligence. It's hard to describe, but it was constant and just underneath the surface. Some situations I encountered were obviously stressful, like when a bullet went racing by my head or a bomb went off in the road ahead of the armored vehicle I was in on my way to the airport. Those incidents are extreme and obvious, but I'm talking about the other times, when stress was more subtle. Former Director George Tenant described it at his retirement ceremony as "carrying a backpack strapped on his back twenty-four-seven."

Director Tenant mentioned he never stopped worrying about the people who worked at the Agency. He felt personally responsible for the security and well-being of all the men and women. His backpack analogy was a great way to describe the underlying stress I felt, especially when I assigned others or was responsible for officers in challenging parts of the world. I often share that there wasn't a night I went to bed, particularly as I got more senior, that I didn't sleep with my phone by my bed. I was on call twenty-four-seven when I had people deployed to conflict zones and living in dangerous places around the world.

I was acutely aware of the long-term effects stress has on a person's health, and I realized I needed to pay attention. I was conscious of what I ate, made sure I exercised regularly, and slept. I may not have been good at it all the time, but they were all the things I tried to do.

I also knew the longer I stayed working with the stress of the CIA, the more likely it would be for me to get sick. Given my family history, I was a good candidate for stress-related illnesses—cancer, heart problems—if I wasn't careful.

I wasn't ready to stop working with the CIA when I became eligible to retire at the age of fifty. Even though I was one of those people that said, "The day I turn fifty, I'm going to retire." I was working with a good team, a great mission, and opportunities to travel to places I hadn't been before. Most importantly, I wasn't sure what I was going to do with my life in my next chapter. These were all good reasons to stick around for a few more years.

I was finishing up a domestic assignment when I was asked to take the director of talent management position for the directorate of support in Langley. I was deeply interested in the position, which had been a dream job of mine for many years, but it would require me to make another move. While I could manage another move, I didn't think I could do justice to the position. To be fair to the director, I would need to be in it for at least three years and work twelve–fourteen-hour days. I knew in my heart I couldn't sustain that pace for another three years without jeopardizing my long-term health.

That's when I decided enough was enough. It was time to retire.

It wasn't an easy decision to make. I had come full circle. I would be leaving all the friends, colleagues, learning, mission focus, and excitement I'd known for thirty-two years.

But there was more to it than that. I was itching to try something new. I wasn't exactly sure what it was going to be, but I was looking for a different kind of challenge. It was time to venture into something where I would have to learn. I also knew I wanted more flexibility in my daily routine and the ability to be selective with whom I worked. I was looking forward to putzing in the morning and going on long walks with Grace.

A friend wisely counseled me to take some "real time off" instead of the three weeks I planned. She explained the science of the brain and how a mind needs rest, especially after the rigors of working at the CIA (Halford 2015). I heeded her advice and took a few months off before I started consulting as a strategic advisor. It was a difficult transition. I was so used to having a packed calendar with not enough hours in a day. Now, when I looked at my calendar and saw a week with no meetings, I would get a pit in my stomach from nerves, thinking, *What am I going to do all day?*

It took me awhile to get used to the new pace. I filled up much of my new free time with hikes and walks with Grace. Time outdoors and in nature was a healing balm. I began writing the *Grace* books, and companies started reaching out to me as word got around that I was consulting.

A few large organizations reached out to me, which helped get me started. I enjoyed those clients, and I'm still with some of them today.

I really didn't know what I was doing when I ventured into my own consulting business, but it was a great opportunity to grow. In the process, I learned a lot about myself. I understood how much I enjoyed working with smart people to transform themselves and their organizations. I also enjoyed using my gift of seeing the big picture while simultaneously understanding what it's going to take to get there.

An important realization I learned through consulting is how much I value the freedom to choose and the ability to leave work in the office.

It is very important for me to grow and to learn. I didn't understand it at the time, but that's what I was doing when I moved into new positions or moved to a new country every three years with the CIA. It's something I continued to do with my *Everybody Loves Grace* books and now with *Humble Yet Fierce.*

CONCLUSION

Humble Yet Fierce

———

When I headed off to college in 1979, I couldn't have imagined that one day I would be writing books and delivering speeches about leadership. Indeed, had you told me I would back then, I would have told you, *"No way!"* both amused and incredulous. Yet you hold in your hands some of my life stories and lessons learned about work and leadership during my thirty-two-year career in the CIA. That was not to be expected from a quiet kid who observed a lot but was unwilling to speak up when the situation warranted it.

Of course, I had a lot of support and help to get to this point. I was blessed to be raised in a solidly middle-class family by loving parents who afforded me the same opportunities for extramural exploration and growth as my four brothers. With respect to career aspirations and dreams, gender was never a consideration. Indeed, my father hoped we would become leaders, whatever the five of us chose to do, and no two of us have pursued a similar career. His only daughter was not exempt. Moreover, he understood to develop as leaders, we would need to make and own consequential decisions concerning the direction of our lives.

Knowing his opinions would likely have undue influence on such decisions, regardless of what he thought might be in our best interest, he generally kept them to himself. Thus, the typical conclusion to requests for advice from him was, "Honey, you'll figure it out. I know you'll make the right decision." That's humble leadership. The longer I live, the more I appreciate his love, faith, and wisdom.

Despite those blessings, I was who I was, and finding my voice has taken most of my adult life. Indeed, the writing of this book revealed to me just how little I had exercised it when I was growing up. Though I wish I had found it sooner, I trust it happened just the way it was supposed to.

Because I was shy, the CIA was a good fit for me. Working behind the scenes doing important work I wasn't allowed to talk about suited me just fine. There were challenges as a woman working in a male-dominated industry, and it took longer for me to progress than my male colleagues. But inspired by good leaders who I tried to emulate throughout my career, I persevered and eventually earned my due.

That personality also shaped my leadership style early in my career. I tried to lead solely by example, speaking up only if I felt there was no other option. Maturing and gaining confidence, I realized speaking up earlier and more often could prevent issues from reaching that point. Make no mistake, learning to trust my voice has been a long process that continues to this day. It can take courage to use it. However, the benefits can be immense.

To steal a quote from George Tenet, "I took the backpack off" when I retired from the CIA.

However, my achievements as a woman and as a leader carried on after I left. It led me to speaking engagements and meaningful interactions with old friends and new friends alike. They encouraged me to share my experiences. I continue to serve the greater good and use it as my north star to guide me, and I've learned to use my voice.

No matter what stage of life I was in, the most effective way for me to lead was with humility. I would "just say yes," and it opened doors for me in unimaginable ways. From saying yes to writing books, the opera, or special assignments with the CIA, every yes created opportunities for me to work on teams with incredibly talented people in interesting places, each with their own unique mission.

One of my key takeaways from leading was I didn't have to be loud to be strong. This attribute caused some people to underestimate me and led to my reputation as someone who was Humble Yet Fierce. I worked with many bosses through the years, and I found the most effective were humble, and I enjoyed working with them the most. They taught me to go where I asked others to go and to laugh at myself along the way, which I do routinely in everyday life.

You don't have to be a CIA station chief or the big cheese to have a good life. But you do need to show up, say yes, have faith, and see where life takes you. You never know, you could watch a concert with royalty, be an extra in an opera, or walk down a dangerous dusty road with a handful of special agents.

Acknowledgments

___

Thank you to the fiercest and most loving support team I could ask for. I want to start with Grace, my faithful companion who sat patiently by my side night after night as I wrote this book. When moments of doubt crept in, she looked at me with her soulful eyes and encouraged me. Her presence made me keep writing.

This book exists because of the people who encouraged me before, during, and after writing it.

It has been my great fortune in writing this book to have my mother encouraging me on. She exemplifies a life lived with strength and courage through adversity, and she passed those lessons on to me.

To my four brothers, thanks for helping me understand what it is to be one of the guys and maintain my femininity. Growing up, you were by my side and taught me how to be tough, independent, and kind.

Beth Nicoson, thank you for never giving up on me. You whispered in my ear for years that I had a story to tell, and here it is.

Linda Hartley, words can't adequately express my gratitude for your thoughtful guidance as I developed the concept and began writing. Your tireless efforts through the revisions and editing process were incredible. I can't imagine writing a book without you on my team.

Cassandra Casswell-Stirling, thank you for urging me on in those difficult moments when I kept saying, "Why didn't I hire a ghostwriter?"

Through it all, I was pushed, coached, charmed, needled, educated, and edited as never before by Maryann Hrichak, Kehkashan Khalid, Michael McQuaid, Katie Mount, Beth Nicoson, and Kathy Waller.

I'm indebted to all those who contributed with quiet encouragement and subtle words of wisdom along the way: Dean Bernard, Dr. Andi Harper, Dr. Hemerson, and Caly Lehrer.

Justine Fedak, I am grateful for a conversation that started with a children's book and ended with you insisting I needed to write about my time in the CIA. I am indebted to you for the title *Humble Yet Fierce.*

A sincere thank you to Eric Koester and the NDP team for guiding me through the process of publishing this book.

To my Author Community, I humbly thank each of you, and the reader, for your belief in me and the story that wanted to be told.

APPENDIX

Central Intelligence Agency. 2013. *Director's Advisory Group on Women in Leadership, Unclassified Report.* Langley, VA: CIA. http://www.cia.gov/readingroom/docs/2013-03-19.pdf.

Prime, Jeanine and Elizabeth Salib. 2014. "Inclusive Leadership: The View from Six Countries." *Research* (blog), *Catalyst.* May 7, 2014. https://www.catalyst.org/research/inclusive-leadership-the-view-from-six-countries/.

CHAPTER 4

Rhimes, Shonda. 2015. *Year of Yes: How to Dance it Out, Stand in the Sun and Be your Own Person.* New York City: Simon and Schuster.

CHAPTER 8

Sinek, Simon (@simonsinek). 2012. "A team is not a group of people that work together. A team is a group of people that *trust* each other." Twitter, August 6, 2012. Accessed January 26, 2023.

CHAPTER 9

George, Bill, and Peter Sims. 2007. *True North, Discover Your Authentic Leadership*. San Francisco: Jossey-Bass.

CHAPTER 24

McQuaid, Katy. 2018. *Everybody Loves Grace: An Amazing True Story of How Grace Brings Love to Everyone She Meets*. Denver: Everybody Loves Grace Publishing.

CHAPTER 26

Pendergast, Alan. 2013. "There's nothing holier-than-thou about Gil Jones." *Longform* (blog), *Westword*. August 22, 2013. https://www.westword.com/news/theres-nothing-holier-than-thou-about-gil-jones-5121710.

Shane, Cari. 2022. "The Psychology Behind Cults." *Mind* (blog), *Discover*. August 16, 2022. https://www.discovermagazine.com/mind/the-psychology-behind-cults.

CHAPTER 29

Halford, Scott. 2015. *Activate Your Brain: How Understanding Your Brain Can Improve Your Work—And Your Life*. Austin: Green Leaf Book Group Press.

Author Bio

Katy McQuaid is an award-winning author and leadership consultant who spent more than three decades in the CIA, including twelve years living abroad. Her work in communities all over the world inspired her to share the art of humble leadership. She is the founder of McQuaid Corporate Performance and Everybody Loves Grace Publishing. A graduate of Penn State University, she attended on a full scholarship, lettered all four years as a swimmer, and earned a Bachelor of Science degree in Finance. Her goal is to support people and organizations in experiencing successful, meaningful, and empowered transformations.

Outside of her work as a consultant and author of the Everybody Loves Grace series, McQuaid is a motivational speaker, writer, and philanthropist. She serves as Chair of the Dorcas Aid America Board of Directors.

Learn more at www.katymcquaid.com and www.everybodylovesgrace.com.